VIS

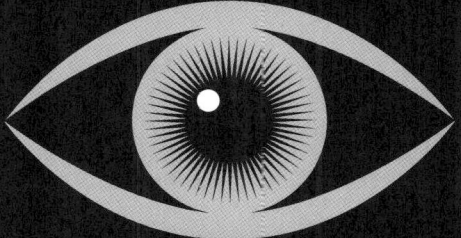

The MIT Press Essential Knowledge Series

A complete list of the titles in this series appears at the back of this book.

VISUAL CULTURE

ALEXIS L. BOYLAN

The MIT Press | Cambridge, Massachusetts | London, England

© 2020 Massachusetts Institute of Technology

All rights reserved. No part of this book may be reproduced in any form by any electronic or mechanical means (including photocopying, recording, or information storage and retrieval) without permission in writing from the publisher.

This book was set in Chaparral Pro by New Best-set Typesetters Ltd. Printed and bound in the United States of America.

Library of Congress Cataloging-in-Publication Data

Names: Boylan, Alexis L., author.
Title: Visual culture / Alexis L. Boylan.
Description: Cambridge, Massachusetts : The MIT Press, [2020] | Series: The MIT Press essential knowledge series | Includes bibliographical references and index.
Identifiers: LCCN 2019058448 | ISBN 9780262539364 (paperback)
Subjects: LCSH: Art and society.
Classification: LCC N72.S6 B595 2020 | DDC 701/.03—dc23
LC record available at https://lccn.loc.gov/2019058448

10 9 8 7 6 5 4 3 2 1

CONTENTS

Series Foreword vii
Acknowledgments ix
Introduction xiii

1 What 1
2 Where 41
3 Who 87
4 When 137
   Conclusion 181

Glossary 187
Notes 193
Further Reading 205
Index 209

SERIES FOREWORD

The MIT Press Essential Knowledge series offers accessible, concise, beautifully produced pocket-size books on topics of current interest. Written by leading thinkers, the books in this series deliver expert overviews of subjects that range from the cultural and the historical to the scientific and the technical.

In today's era of instant information gratification, we have ready access to opinions, rationalizations, and superficial descriptions. Much harder to come by is the foundational knowledge that informs a principled understanding of the world. Essential Knowledge books fill that need. Synthesizing specialized subject matter for nonspecialists and engaging critical topics through fundamentals, each of these compact volumes offers readers a point of access to complex ideas.

ACKNOWLEDGMENTS

To begin, the most profound and heartfelt thanks to Victoria Hindley for finding me. Then, after she found me, she was impossibly inspiring and challenging. Her vision, generosity, and kindness are epic, and I feel very lucky to have circled into her orbit. Thank you.

Brilliant, inspired colleagues and friends listened, read, offered ideas, and aided every page; they include Betsy Athens, Viola Augustin, Matthew Baigell, Thomas Baione, Deirdre Bair, Brian Bishop, Anna Mae Duane, Jonathan Entis, Anke Finger, Robin Greeley, Susan Herbst, Kathy Knapp, Bill McCarty, Adam McGee, Michael Orwicz, Melina Pappademos, Janet Pritchard, Mai Reitmeyer, Rebecca Segal, Christine Sylvester, Martina Tanga, Scott Wallace, and Edvin Yegir. Great thanks are also owed to the whole UConn Humanities Institute team—Nasya Al-Saidy, Yohei Igarashi, Michael P. Lynch, Siavash Samei, and Jo-Ann Waide—who gave me precious time and space to write, encouraged me, and generally helped lighten the load in crucial moments. Thank you again. Additionally, the team at MIT made writing this book a dream; special thanks to Matthew Abbate and Gabriela Bueno Gibbs who are both so dreamy and so talented.

Crucial support, humor, and goodwill were provided by James Ouellette and Melanie Chebro. I would also like to thank the Inter-Library Loan team at UConn and then the librarians at the Cambridge Public Library–Central Square Branch. Nothing would have happened without their help. Thanks too for the time and thoughtfulness of the outside reviewers of this book, including Lisa Cartwright. Their time and thoughtful engagement are deeply appreciated, and hopefully they can read their improvements throughout the text. Several artists and scholars extended great generosity in allowing their work to be shown in this book, including Morehshin Allahyari, Brian Bishop, Han Seok Hyun, Valerie Hegarty, Jacqui Kenny, Emilio Madrid-Kuser, Emily Moore, Jennifer Steinkamp, and Scott Wallace. It is an honor to share space with your images.

Funding that supported this book's illustrations and other materials was provided through research support from Dean Anne D'Alleva, School of Fine Arts, Dean Juli Wade, former Dean Davita Silfen Glasberg, and Associate Dean Cathy Schlund-Vials, all of the College of Liberal Arts and Sciences, and from the Office of the Provost, University of Connecticut. Their collective advocacy of scholarship in the arts and humanities is deeply valued. Many thanks.

Ethan Seidman again helped me focus on what is important. Thank you. I owe a great debt to my colleague and friend Kelly Dennis who helped in editing the book, making it infinitely better. Thanks to my family (including

Busy) for their support, love, and patience. Gabe Boylan lovingly read, argued, and pushed me to be smarter and bolder, a task he has done in this book but also in life and for which I am endlessly grateful.

Finally, all the love—far beyond what the eye can see—to Micki McElya.

INTRODUCTION

Naiveté is often the excuse for those who exercise power. For those upon whom that power is exercised, naiveté is always a mistake.

Michel-Rolph Trouillot[1]

Pink or blue? Animals or abstract patterns? Overstuffed or austere?

The various hopes, traps, anticipations, and anxieties of the visual are perhaps most obviously apparent in Western baby instruction manuals and parenting books. These books—really all parenting advice, especially in the United States—are the great tells of any community and neatly capture its pressure points, dreams, aspirations, and fears, which have little to do with babies and everything to do with the adults around them.

Visual environments are *very* important in contemporary parenting books. To have a mobile or not, the number of stuffed animals, what colors, what shapes—all become codes for:

I love my child.

I want them to be successful.

I can soothe, shape, and protect them.

Above all, I can make them be like me.

For newborns, parents are encouraged to create the perfect balance of colorful and engaging, though not *too* stimulating, or the baby will never sleep. As the babies grow, parents are counseled that toddlers need bold colors; blue and green can calm whereas red and orange will excite the imagination—but might also be agitating. White is soothing, but may also seem clinical. Accents can help—but be careful, not too much!

And then there is gender. Blue in modern commercial culture has been associated with boys and male energy, while pink has been associated with girls and the feminine. This is often one of the first community and family decisions new parents make: do they capitulate to these traditional gendered visual schemes, or steer clear of them with theoretically gender-neutral colors like green and yellow? What if friends or family give their child gender-specific clothes or toys, or pictures to hang on the walls? Maybe it will hurt, maybe it will punish the child and undermine their self-esteem, or maybe it will be meaningless, lost, and quickly forgotten. Surely there are bigger, more pressing issues at hand; but it's your child's development, identity, and wellbeing on the line. These crucial and fundamental moments could start them down a path of pain. Visual culture is frivolous, trivial, indulgent, even incidental, until it is life-altering, traumatizing, violent, and deadly.

As the toddler becomes a child and then a teenager, each stage is curated with color and design, shifting the visual environment. Older children are aged out of pastels and promoted to primary colors. Why? Who made these visual rules? When, exactly, does a child grow into navy or maroon? What is the rationale behind that transition, and how does a parent know when to make it? Shouldn't there be bigger concerns? By the same token, there are seldom babies dressed in all black, tucked into a black crib, snuggled into black blankets. In Western cultures this would seem ghoulish, too much association with death and darkness and other qualities deemed at odds with how children should be.

The scientific evidence for claims about visual culture in child development might be specious, but a lot of time, money, energy, and emotion are spent—and historically have been spent—crafting the perfect visual environments so that children can grow to be the adults their parents want them to be. This preoccupation reveals both a hopefulness for and significant anxiety about the power of the visual. There is no end of examples of how visual objects have been used to influence, narrate, hide, and reveal. As a child's environment is arranged to exhibit the parents' values and to mirror parental identities, so, too, is our larger visual culture curated to create desired outcomes.

That's a lot of passive-voice verb use. Who is curating that "larger visual culture" and what, exactly, are the desired outcomes?

Visual imagery swirls around us, some of it invited but most of it not. All these visual objects, the additions and the things omitted, create a visual environment where all the little pieces we see (colors, animals, the moon, skyscrapers, stop signs, political flyers, Kim Kardashian West) become (1) legible, (2) naturalized, normalized, and made obvious, and (3) mapped and accessible. How does this happen, and then how do we live and move in our visual environments? How do we confront "new" objects, and how do we integrate them into the lexicon of images we already "know"?

Optimists might view visual culture as a way to create individual identities and collective belonging, as a means to find joy or balance, peace, and hope. They might view a visual atmosphere as being like a giant department store in which they are customers, free to pick and choose items that best reflect them and their values. In this scenario, we are always the boss, always in control, always aware of options, able to negotiate and contain our environments and our own responses to them. We are free agents making choices. Collectively we are a collaborative visual team, passing images back and forth to each other, rejecting and accepting, and thus the curators of our own lives.

An optimist might also look at visual culture as an opportunity to seed the world with good ideas and creativity, and to mitigate antisocial behaviors. This is exactly what parents try to do with a baby's visual environment—make it a place where a baby can thrive, in the ways a parent values and recognizes. Likewise, a Japanese garden is styled to make a specific visual impression, and these are not surface-level, random, or merely pleasing choices. Each decision about materials and arrangement in a space is made with the aim of creating a holistic, immersive experience that generates specific ideas, relations, and feelings about nature, the self, and the interrelation of objects, beings, and space. And all of these decisions mean different things if we are thinking of an Edo period (1603–1868) garden, a garden in a mall in contemporary Tokyo, or a garden in a trendy neighborhood in Berlin. The visual can and does morph and reassemble in generative and inspiring ways. Visual culture is a place of possibility, of peace, of community, and of creativity.

Then there are the other, darker dialogues about visual culture in this historical moment, suggesting its more ominous and violent potentials. You might, for example, hear about paintings that sell for ever higher amounts of money, and wonder why it is harder than ever to assess the value of art, what it means, and to whom. More unsettling might be our subjection to an endless deluge of violent images and a fear that this reflects general public callousness to violence, cruelty, and sadism. Or you might be uncomfortable thinking about CCTV in public spaces and the various security cameras tracking us, not to mention drones that can spy on anyone, anywhere. It is hard also not to fear facial recognition software that will make each of us instantly and constantly trackable, or deep fakes and AI-generated images. Museums where black children are assaulted with racial slurs from other patrons and followed by security guards might seem the exact opposite of what those institutional spaces are for. #Metoo has made consuming some films, television programs, and other visual products impossible, guilt-inducing, or uncomfortable. Images and art that once promised and even delivered glorious pleasure, escape, or profound insights might now bring sadness or defensiveness. And is anything we see real? Manipulation of photographs and of all things digital is old news, but the refinement of 3D technology promises to make most objects infinitely replicable, obscuring even further the notions of an original and its copies, the real and the fakes. None of us are likely to own our faces or bodies in the future; in fact, many of us have already (willingly or unknowingly) given our faces to Google, Facebook, dating and hookup apps, and the government.

From the pessimist side, visual culture can be understood as a rich garden of disaster and despair. How can we not get overwhelmed and dragged under by it all? How can we refrain from paranoia and the fear of technology and change while being vigorous, persistent, and even merciless in confronting climate collapse, structural inequality, and the compounding injustices of our historical moment? How do we resist the manipulations of the state, global corporate interests, and other powerful actors that seek to dominate our visual field? How do we curate our own visual atmospheres while allowing others to curate theirs? What is our moral obligation to witness, and when is it ethical to look away and reject seeing?

This book is structured to give some space, context, history, examples, and momentum as one confronts these questions. What I hope it will offer are pathways, critiques, some tools, a bit of fear, a bit more of solace, and much more power in *your* ability to look and to see differently. While historically the visual environment has always been important, it goes without saying that technology has shifted its global stakes. The visual moves now along fundamentally different pathways, and while I would argue this hasn't shifted the substance of the visual, it has shifted the density, reach, and immediacy of visual culture. This is to say, visual culture is not merely an important feature of contemporary life; it is the *most important* culture we must navigate. We are forced to *see* more yet given fewer tools and less time to *think about seeing*. If we cannot stop the pace of images, if we cannot remove ourselves from the pipeline of contemporary living, then we must carve out spaces to think, debate, and come to terms with this visual world. This book is a tool for that project.

To put it another way, this book aims to help manage and confront what the visual does more than settle on fixed definitions of what it is. Thus, while the book will

Visual culture is not merely an important feature of contemporary life; it is the *most important* culture we must navigate.

touch upon contested definitions of "art," "value," and "taste," it won't invest much energy in parsing or stabilizing those categories. Instead, we'll consider the greater benefit and experimental possibility to be found in engaging more voices. I want us all to be more engaged viewers, to understand how our social, cultural, geographical, and temporal locations shape our ways of seeing. More engagement means more aggressively confronting the ethics of looking and of seeing, while at the same time remaining open to visual diversity, discomfort, and surprising delight; to feel all the pleasure, sadness, and grace the visual can offer.

This is hard work, requiring the curious looker to negotiate a range of competing positions on the visual. In the early twentieth century, Italian futurists, who were contemporaries of French cubist painters, were committed to new and modern ways of seeing the world. In their quest to realize (their version of) a better visual culture, the futurists demanded to "destroy the museums, libraries, academies of every kind."[2] The impulse has logic, for it is not just technology that has made the visual such a minefield but history as well. We are surrounded by objects and visuals from the past that haunt us or that we can't let go.

There has always been deep conflict about the meaning of images, about their authority and that of their producers and consumers, about who is seen and in what ways. On the one hand, there has been a persistent confidence in the visual as a pathway to belonging, knowledge, and power, one encouraged—sometimes incrementally, at other times through vast campaigns—by governments, religious authorities, monarchs, mass media, artists, corporate entities, and various public and private cultural institutions. Technology only strengthened the idiom, with photography, film, satellites, X-rays, and microscopic imagery all empowering scientific theory and thought, which furthered the idea that the visual was true and verified science and that science, in turn, confirmed the veracity of the visual. If the visual has been looked to as a pathway to truth and knowledge, it has just as often been understood as a treacherous road to deception, falsehoods, and fakery.

Mastery and control over the visual are advocated by many, but censorship, limiting screen time, and banning violent video games are not the answers advocated here. In this book, together with many scholarly and artistic voices, we will examine our and others' visual wants and needs across space and time to understand the viciousness, power, individual pleasures, and potential public good the visual holds. We will explore how people are shaped and policed through visual culture, by the images we seek out and choose to see, those we have no control over, and those we are refused access to.

Visual culture is never neutral, and is thus never without value. Visual culture is power. As historian

Visual culture is never neutral, and is thus never without value. Visual culture is power.

Michel-Rolph Trouillot might say, none of us can afford to be naive and just hope for the best where visual culture is concerned. The visual always *means* something.

That's what this book confronts. How can we shape a better visual culture and build better futures? How can we create visual atmospheres that are livable for most people most of the time? Can visual culture save us from ourselves? Who gets to be the "we," "us," and self-possessed if imperiled "ourselves" in this equation?

Fortunately, faced with these questions many brilliant scholars, artists, and critics have offered suggestions, solutions, and possibilities, some of which are reviewed in this book. This book offers a chance to walk together and consider the sadness and fear as well as the inspiring potential of visual culture. It is my hope that by the end we will quite literally *see better*, not merely with more attention to detail or more information and facts, but with mission confidence, and with more wonder and respect for the power of the visual to shape justice, history, and values. I hope we can reject naiveté to embrace our own authority and engage the power of the visual.

The book is organized as a map for navigating the winding and complex issues of visual culture. We won't start with cave paintings and end with contemporary art, and the goal is not to see some objects as "old" and others as "modern." Instead, the four chapters encourage considering the visual as clusters of mechanisms and strategies that humans use to locate the "what," "who," "where," and "when" of our existence.

Each chapter begins with a "Provocation." These visual case studies describe an object or incident and its multiple and often competing interpretations as a way to introduce the chapter's themes. The provocations provide an opportunity for you to locate your own wants and preconceptions about an issue or objects, encouraging you to think through your position, your priorities, and your gut feeling about an issue and then consider whether your ideas and feelings have shifted by the time you reach the end of the chapter. Shifting is not necessarily the goal, but participation is. Visual culture demands attention. This book offers tools to help you look with critical attention and find a path to what you want or need from visual culture.

The first chapter, "What," takes on the question: What is visual culture? What questions and ideas animate how we approach the visual? What is it that we want in thinking about visual culture? What possibilities and pitfalls lurk as we critically engage visual culture? Many people want many things from visual objects, and visual objects want things right back. "What" considers how the visual has been organized as knowledge, what tensions this produces, and what potential there might be in thinking through visual culture.

The place one stands in the world has been crucial to what one sees. The second chapter maps this "Where" in regard to our visual culture, visual environment, and visual atmosphere. What are we allowed to see? Where are we allowed to see it? What is inside visual culture and what is outside? In confronting these questions, we consider ideas about art, the history and purpose of museums, and what powers are invested in sustaining an inside and outside in visual culture. Indeed the deeper problem may be that there is no inside or outside. Visual culture might not be here, or there, but it is increasingly important to know where we stand.

The third chapter, "Who," considers the human body and how historically and in the contemporary moment various bodies and identities have been present or absent from visual culture. More perplexing is the question about whether anyone's body can be excused from the visual culture party. *Who* have we been looking at, and what have we been seeing? Is there a way to see race, gender, sexuality, ability, and all the other ways our bodies are categorized anew, or is visual culture just a loop of alienation and injustice?

The last chapter, "When," moves us to how we see the temporal change embedded in nature, landscapes, and the environment. Creating a stable geography, a knowable visual space, mapping time itself have been a fixation in the visual sphere. We think we are mapping a "where," but we are really visualizing a "when." The ocean, the animals, outer space, all have been drawn and redrawn, imagined, categorized, and visually quantified, often detached from the "when" and placed in a non-time. But all this loving attention seems at odds with what many have argued is a current inability to speak with visual clarity and power to the *when* of climate change, extinctions, pollution, and the other evidences of environmental devastation. What might it mean if visual culture cannot be mobilized to address the most altering events in the story of humanity?

Confronting the visual atmosphere is of profound importance now. Artist and theorist Allan deSouza notes that "a book does not mark the end of a project but its entry into public dialogue."[3] Let us see together what we can find.

1

WHAT

Provocation

So much art disappears, so much visual culture seems to just slip away into the ether. Some ends violently—beaten, burned, stolen, abandoned, innocent victim of crossfire in a battle, executed publicly for its crimes. Many such works are deeply missed; people go looking for them, try to nurse them back to health, or stage a memorial.

Other works disappear the same way they were created, with little fanfare, no notice, and no one there to celebrate or mourn. Some visual images are loved, most are not.

King Uthal is part of a work by Morehshin Allahyari titled *Material Speculation: ISIS* from 2015. Allahyari defines herself as an artist, activist, writer, and educator, and her work has been featured in numerous international

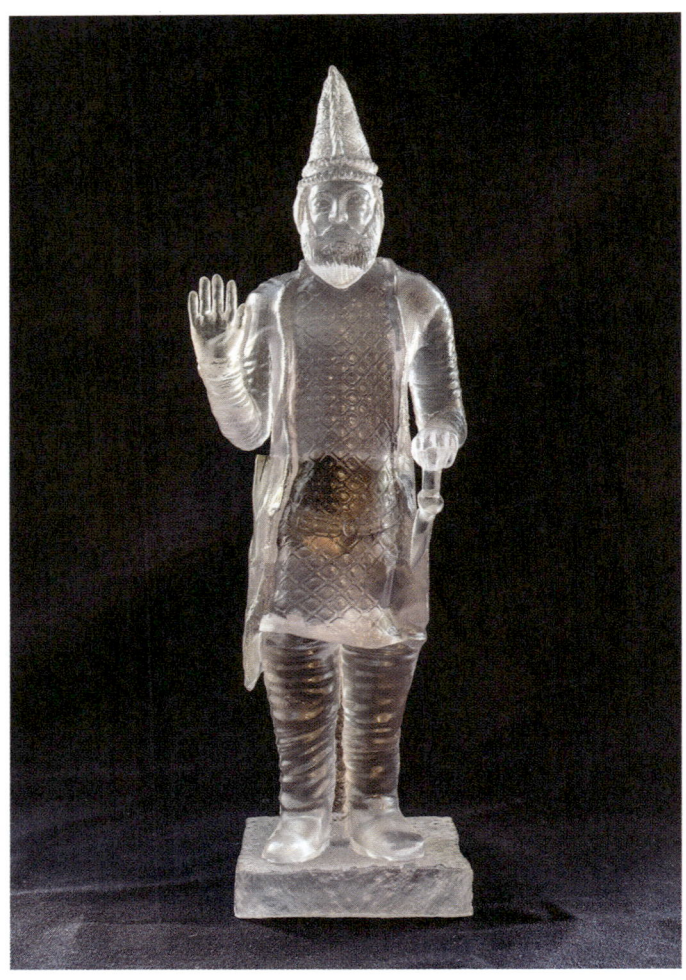

Figure 1 Morehshin Allahyari, *King Uthal*, 2015. 3D-printed resin and electronic components, 12 × 4 × 3½ in. (30.5 × 10.2 × 8.9 cm). Image courtesy of the artist and Upfor Gallery, shot by Mario Gallucci.

biennials and in numerous museum collections. Made of clear plastic with a 3D printer, this is a replica of a sculpture once held at the Mosul Museum, the second largest museum in Iraq. Very little is known about the original sculpture; the work is associated with the city of Hatra in northern Iraq and believed to be from between the first century BCE and the second century CE. There is minimal information about who King Uthal was or the circumstances, function, or original location of the work.

When ISIS seized Mosul in 2015, they broadcast their victory by creating a video of fighters smashing the sculpture of King Uthal, along with several other objects in the museum. The video was part of a wider communications campaign aimed at shocking the enemies of ISIS in Iraq and around the world, particularly the West, and recruiting more fighters. The recorded destruction was also an overt attempt to silence a history of Iraq that was not Islamic—to destroy a past, and a culture, literally and then figuratively.[1]

Allahyari's piece might be taken simply and powerfully as an act of reclamation or restoration, as a recreation of the destroyed work in exacting detail through 3D printing technology. Her replica might be seen as mourning the original sculpture while attempting to undo the violence that was perpetrated against it. The replica could be seen as reversing time, returning power to the object in its wholeness (as opposed to fragmentation).

Yet such a reading would not be an accurate or complete description either of this piece or of Allahyari's larger project, *Material Speculation*, of which *King Uthal* is one element. While exhibiting the 3D-printed works in a gallery, Allahyari simultaneously made her "original" files available in "The Download" space of the online journal *Rhizome*. The journal encourages readers to download files in order to create their own exhibitions. In the case of *Material Speculation*, Allahyari made her entire work available for download as a zip file (still available online in January 2020). The kit includes the technical specifications needed for 3D printing; academic articles, historical museum catalogues, ephemera, and videos about the "original" works in the Mosul Museum; the ISIS-produced footage of their destruction in 2015; journalistic accounts and US and Iraqi governmental reports about the destruction; and email exchanges between Allahyari and museum staff and others about the sculptures.[2]

By disseminating the work online as information, the artist creates neither a replica of the ancient work nor something original. Instead she activates the dispersal of information, visual objects, and data that cannot be contained in their distribution or their meanings. Anyone with access to a 3D printer can make a *King Uthal*, multiplying the disappeared object's availability and thus diminishing significantly its "original" value. The *King Uthal* sculpture is gone forever, yet exists as an endlessly replicable object in perpetuity (as long as there are computers and compatible printing technology).

Rather than privilege the historical, the original, or the singular artwork by mourning its destruction, might Allahyari's act in fact demonstrate the ability of technology to eradicate all "originals"? By diluting ISIS's "shock-and-awe" powers of destruction, is she not also stripping power from *all* of the institutions built to control imagery, its value, and its circulation? In other words, Allahyari could be viewed as seeking to liberate all images from ISIS, from the US government, from museums, galleries, and from any other institutional interference to the movement of visual data. The gesture also suggests that the role of the artist, and indeed of all of us, is not to create "originals" of anything but to move data.

Material Speculation in turn was part of a larger project in which Allahyari joined with artist Daniel Rourke to explore and exploit the radical potential of new technologies (such as 3D printing) for the purpose of creating a new vision of existence. The core of this investigation is the term "Additivism," which Allahyari and Rourke describe as "a portmanteau of **additive** and **activism**: a gesture to the complex scales at which new forms of action and intervention must take place in an era increasingly saturated by PostHuman affects."[3]

Additivism can emancipate us.

Additivism will eradicate us.

We want to encourage, interfere, and reverse-engineer the possibilities encoded into the censored, the invisible, and the radical notion of the 3D printer itself.

Creation must be a violent assault on the forces of matter, to extrude its shape and extract its raw potential.

For only Additivism can accelerate us to an aftermath whence **all** matter has mutated into the clarity of plastic.[4]

King Uthal was an element, an activated agent of this call to arms, a call to use both Western ideas about art and originality and a faith in technology as weapons to end this world and make a new one. As scholars Alexis Anais Avedisian and Anna Khachiyan argued, the objects created from this toxic plastic play with their own villainy. "In such a way, the *3D Additivist Manifesto* goes beyond revealing the electronic processes that make tangible products out of digitally rendered models, it fundamentally attempts to expose histories that have been concealed in service of upholding the hyperfiction that technology is a cure-all for the world's social and economic ills."[5] The violence against the original *King Uthal* was reproduced by means of visual technologies: the resurrection of *King Uthal* was another form of violence done via the visual to diminish the authority of both humans and machines.

In the end, it is unclear whether Allahyari's *King Uthal* works to honor, replace, remember, and mourn a lost work from the Mosul Musuem by giving it back some presence and physicality, or whether this reincarnation has made *King Uthal* so clear and transparent that we can no longer register it.

Who wants what?

I want to go to the movies.

I want to look at the animals at the zoo.

I want to see the exhibition.

I want to wear new clothes.

I want to see the stars.

I want to wear this concert T-shirt.

I want to hang that on my wall.

I want you to send me that picture.

This chapter looks to explore the *what* of visual culture: What is it? What is the history of visual culture? What ideas or philosophies does "visual culture" encompass? What are the limits of visual culture?

To get to these questions, it is important to first consider what we each bring to the visual. What are the experiences, emotions, and positions or stabilities we seek when we look at or see things? To get to *what* visual culture is, we must first consider what we want from it.

As even that very short list suggests, as viewers we *want a lot* from the visual. It could be argued that humans have, in fact, for a long time wanted way too much from the visual. There are traces of this wanting on the walls of caves, in carved sculptures, in stacked stones, and in traces drawn around human hands. The wanting intensified as skills, tools, and technology to produce—and reproduce—images became more sophisticated. Whenever we can, wherever we are, we want images. We crave representation, repetition, and the possibility of making our mark. As much as we hunger for some images, we also want very much *not to see* others. We desire to see and we reject seeing. In this sense, little has changed since our ancestors began stacking stones, creating scrolls, and first pondering the creative abilities of artificial intelligence.

What is it, then, that pulls us—in all places, at every time, in each stage of life, and in ever-increasing varieties—to images? Perhaps we seek solace, or to communicate emotions, fears, and ideas we find difficult to put into words. We want to confront death, we want to avoid

As much as we hunger for some images, we also want very much *not to see* others. We desire to see and we reject seeing.

death, we want to stop time, we want beauty, we want to see suffering and how brutal life can be, we want to be converted, to drop to our knees and cry with joy, we want to see the land, we want to see the land we cannot see, we want to see the stars and beyond them, we want to laugh, we want to see how meaningless we are, we want to know how important and full of grace we are, we want to imagine who or what made us, we want to see how little we can see. The depth of our wanting is bottomless and our reasons endless. The only stable constant across space and time is the wanting itself.

This human wanting is old. But a more pernicious idea has recently been added to the mix: what does the visual want from us? Visual theorist W. J. T. Mitchell posed this question in his book *What Do Pictures Want? The Lives and Loves of Images* (2005). He framed his provocative query through a fact that producers of visual culture have long understood: if the human hand makes images, it almost simultaneously loses control of those images, unleashing them to a future beyond any individual's command. The ancient Greek myth of Pygmalion describes a sculptor who falls so in love with the idealized woman of his creation that the goddess of love, Aphrodite, makes the piece real: awakened with a kiss, the sculpture then bears the sculptor a child.[6] While the myth of Pygmalion and Galatea might be read as an allegory of human wanting from images, it is, in fact, a story of an image come to life,

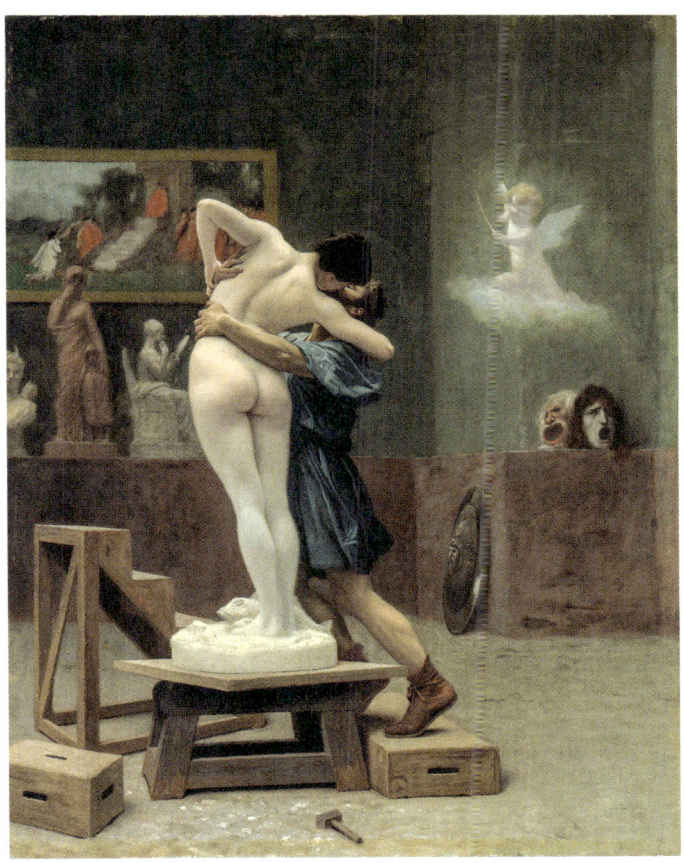

Figure 2 Jean-Léon Gérôme, *Pygmalion and Galatea* ca. 1890. Oil on canvas. Metropolitan Museum of Art, New York.

and even reproducing life. The object, made for one purpose, takes on a story and narrative arc of its own. The sculpture evolves and desires things, too.

The dogged way that images take on lives of their own comprises, as Mitchell suggests, what images *want*. For life in all its forms seems to be about wanting, whether or not that wanting is conscious: the need to reproduce or imprint, to strategically call attention to or hide, to shift and change in different geographic or material circumstances, to age, to move—all are needs images can manifest. But more than these needs, it is the hunger to speak, to communicate, to convince that makes images most lifelike. If people want from images, images appear to want things, too; and the wants of the two are not always in concert.

Pygmalion begins as a story of love but becomes a story of obsession, of being overtaken by an image, and of the capacity of images to isolate people from one another. Without the gift of Aphrodite, we are left to imagine only isolation in Pygmalion's future, a slow disintegration of the self, and perhaps, in the end, even madness. Or perhaps the subject of the story isn't really Pygmalion at all but Galatea. She is given the gift of agency by Aphrodite. She was made to be wanted; that desire, Pygmalion's kiss, awakens her wants, and the child she bears is born wanting.

To complicate this issue of wanting and ownership even further, we now live at a time when the maker or artist or craftsperson—whatever you want to call them—might not be *a person* at all, but a string of code. More and more of the images that we see daily, images that we rely on to tell us crucial information about our bodies, about where we are, about what the galaxy looks like, are not "made" in any conventional sense. Computers turn data into visuals, programming shifts color and line in Photoshop without any human guidance, images of unknown origin are sent to us and posted for and by us.[7] Often their origins are not human. And even if the image in question was made by a human at some point, that touch becomes lost in the mix. As artist Cory Arcangel has noted, "When I put something on my blog, no one knows I'm an artist. As soon as it gets copied and pasted to another blog, I cease to become an artist. It just becomes another piece of information on the net."[8] This, too, begs the question: What do technology, computers, and other nonhuman visual creators want from us?[9]

The visual is part of a story that humans weave, but humans are also parts in the narrative created by images. Our wanting gives way to the fact that we are all pulled into the visual, summoned to dance together. In writing about the terrible persistence of images of black enslavement and torture, scholar Saidiya Hartman argues that visual culture knits together people across time and space. "What interests me," she writes, "are the ways in which we are called upon to participate in such scenes."[10] The visual implicates us, makes us witnesses, puts us on notice, engages us in ways we might very much not want, but are compelled to regardless.[11]

This was demonstrated in 2018 when the national government of Brazil, under the auspices of Fundação Nacional do Índio (FUNAI), released video footage of the last surviving member of an uncontacted tribe in the Amazon.[12] The film was created by a group of government officials tasked with maintaining the man's safety by protecting him from those who might stumble upon or willingly seek to find him, communicate with him, or hurt him. In the name of his protection, the man was being tracked, filmed, and watched without his knowledge. (A note to the reader: this image is of an abandoned canoe left by members of another uncontacted Amazonian tribe, the Flecheiros. I wanted to give a visual aid here, but did not want to implicate the book in repeating the images of the video.)

The video quality was crude, constantly zooming in and out of focus. The man appears in the distance, busy at work chopping a tree. Little can be ascertained about his individual features, but he appears to be struggling with physically demanding work. The video then becomes confusing, with the camera losing focus and dropping away from the man entirely for a moment. The chopping continues, but it takes a few more seconds for the camera to return to the star of the show. This disturbance, however accidental and unartful, serves to remind the viewer of the act of watching. The viewer is denied the main attraction,

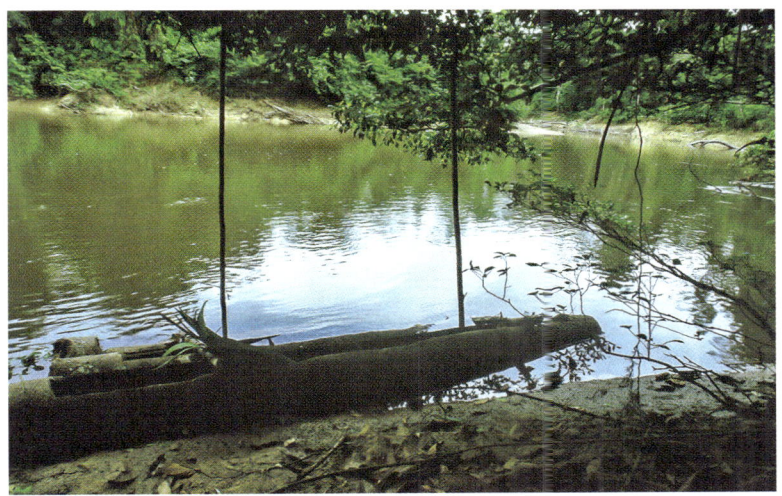

Figure 3 Scott Wallace, *Flecheiros Canoe*, 2002. Photography. Image courtesy of the artist.

which frustrates and feeds the urge to see again. The filming realigns, and for several moments the focus gets closer and then retreats. Whispers of the cameramen can be heard, urging to "zoom-zoom-zoom." All the while, the man keeps chopping. Then, without the tree dropping, he walks away and the film cuts. It lasts less than a minute and a half, and was viewed over 3 million times on YouTube.

Even the comments posted on YouTube noted that it was "mad to think that he is blissfully unaware of over a million people around the world watching him via technology that he has no idea that exists."[13] Yet watched this solitary man was; over and over, without his permission, without his consultation, and without any significant moral debate. He is the last of his tribe, and the global audience is told that all we can do is watch. What does the popularity of this particular video say about a global fascination with visibility and invisibility, power and powerlessness, technology, extinction, and notions of the antimodern? Why have audiences been so compelled to watch this particular man, amidst all the other content competing for their attention?

Likely in response to the popularity of the footage, FUNAI released another short video a few weeks later. This one was filmed by a drone and shows members of a different uncontacted tribe. Several figures move across the landscape, the drone focusing its gaze on the bodies as they slip in and out of sightlines hindered by foliage. This video received almost 5 million views, and outlets such as the BBC and *National Geographic* featured articles and showed the video over and over, freezing frames and zooming in on the unknowing men and women deep in the Amazon.

Is seeing innocent? When does seeing become an act of violence or aggression? What rights do any of us have to be seen or not to be seen, to make ourselves invisible?

The videos exist, at least according to FUNAI, as part of their work to protect indigenous people and tribal cultures. Releasing the short films was necessary, they claimed, "to heighten awareness within Brazil and around the world of the existence of the isolated tribes and their increasingly precarious status."[14] From this perspective, visual images are agents of safety, and morally necessary to accomplish a higher calling. If we follow the logic of those who distributed the video, it is innocent, as are the people who made it and the people who watch it. All are free of blame, as the real enemies are out there, unseen, but ready to exploit or harm the uncontacted—the visual has been weaponized for good. It is not a stretch to argue, from this point of view, that the most *ethical and moral* thing a global audience could do in that moment is to watch.

FUNAI could easily call upon this narrative, and a global audience could so quickly accept it, because its rationale was not novel. It is the one governments have used in emergencies, such as in the United States after 9/11, to point cameras at public streets, to send drones to the edges of the earth to see what "terrorists" are up to, and to secretly monitor the internet use, the YouTube and Google searches, of its citizens. Protection is the language of the security state.

Almost a year after Brazil released its videos, a different sort of weaponization of the visual took place. In the context of fraught public debates about immigration, amidst daily reports of children being separated from their parents and locked in makeshift holding pens at the United States-Mexico border, journalists were tipped off to a private Facebook site for United States Customs and Border Patrol (CBP) agents. The site, which had almost 10,000 members, was aimed at insider humor and community-building for CBP agents. But numerous posts featured visuals of dead migrants, photographs that had first been featured in mainstream news outlets but were here given new "joke" captions. There were also a number of photographs of Representative Alexandra Ocasio-Cortez that had been manipulated to be sexually explicit.[15]

The posts were exposed because they were not deemed innocent by those outside the CPB, which quickly disavowed them as the work of a few bad apples. The press swarmed and opinion pieces raged. Images were now the guilty party, the bad omen, the representation of an evil. Much particular ire was directed at an image of a drowned man and his young child that featured on the CBP agents' Facebook site, their bodies washed up on the bank of the stretch of river they had been attempting to cross. Again, this was not the first viewing of this photograph; it had been widely distributed as an illustration of the immigration crisis in newspaper articles and op-ed pieces decrying US immigration policies and the inhumane conditions at the southern border. The image itself was unchanged from the news to the Facebook post, only the context and more importantly the intent had changed. Where does that leave the image? Guilty or innocent?

As with the images of indigenous people in the Brazilian rainforest, no one gave permission to reproduce pictures of dead migrants and asylum seekers, just as Ocasio-Cortez did not give permission to have her likeness morphed into a picture of her fellating a migrant.

Permission doesn't matter much. At some point, access and surveillance have become ubiquitous. We assume that all have the power to look, and that someone always has the power to look at us. When used for "good"—to warn people, to teach people, to signal empathy—images are innocent allies. But presumably these same images can switch teams, to violate, expose, or incite people.

How are we to think about the guilt or innocence of the visual in any given situation? Can the visual ever be counted on to do what is right? Can we even ask such a thing of it? Or is the visual always a tool of violence, violation, or transgression? Who among us gets to decide?

This is precisely the issue that Hartman was highlighting in her suggestion that we are "called to participate." We might want images to behave in certain ways, but they won't. And what is wanted from images keeps shifting and changing. How can we find some terra firma in this unsteady terrain?

This is where critical and scholarly theories about visual culture can help.

What is visual culture?

Questions about consent, diversity, authority, invisibility, and rights have become particularly urgent in recent decades, signaling what many scholars call the "philosophical turn" in the study of the visual.[16] The philosophical turn locates images within more far-reaching disciplinary and ideological terrains. The big questions, in other words, are not merely about interpretation but philosophy and values; they ask how the visual has been organized as knowledge and plumb the tensions that knowledge produces. A renewed interest in visual culture just shows that we were always talking about wanting, about guilt and innocence, about who owns all these ideas, and what might be the best way to confront them.

Visual culture as a field of study and academic discipline is relatively new. Yet, while it has grown into its own disciplinary location, many would argue it is less a field than an attitude, a way of thinking and looking, or a means of inclusion unbound by disciplinary convention. We'll start with a very abbreviated history of the growth of visual culture studies to set the contours of this intellectual dialogue and then consider how this scholarly turn can help us navigate the visual in a more lived and perhaps less academic sense.

Pinpointing origins or getting *the exact moment* when an idea or discipline is born has a nice efficiency to it. We

The big questions are not merely about interpretation but philosophy and values; they ask how the visual has been organized as knowledge and plumb the tensions that knowledge produces.

could start with "a meeting here" or "an essay there" and then move on in an orderly chronological fashion to specific authors, noteworthy texts, and canonical moments. Yet, as we will discuss, canons are part of the very problem that visual culture studies seeks to dismantle. Additionally, as the scholar Donna Haraway notes, "an origin story in the 'Western,' humanist sense depends on the myth of original unity, fullness, bliss and terror."[17] The visual and culture have never been that neat, and myths, according to Haraway, only take us farther from where we need to go.

Thus, it is fitting that there is no consensus about when visual culture studies began. Some scholars place it in the 1990s with the end of the Cold War; others push its beginnings earlier to the 1980s with the growth of media studies and shifting ideas about aesthetics influenced by the intellectual energy of late 1960s radicalism and reorderings inspired by postmodernism, multiculturalism, and feminism; or they look earlier still, to the popular works of philosopher Marshall McLuhan. Others locate the young field as a direct response to postcolonial scholars and broad pressures on institutional disciplinarity and knowledge production.[18]

If we cannot specify a birth date, we can identify some of the places the conversation started. Art history has been the traditional disciplinary location dedicated to the study of art, artists, style, and the meanings and power of images and iconography. Art history's origins are tightly woven with notions of creativity, genius, and the artist in Western European culture, nurtured by the Enlightenment ideals of categorization and progression.[19] The field of study grew from the philosophical insights of Immanuel Kant, Georg Hegel, and Martin Heidegger but took shape as its own discipline and methodology.[20] The conversation turned from the philosophical back to the object and to practices of close looking, working to define beauty, quality, chronology, and form. Critic Walter Benjamin expanded the dialogue in the early twentieth century with his arguments about film, spectatorship, and "mechanical reproducibility."[21] He challenged the narrow focus on objects while inspiring even greater attention to them. Benjamin's theories about the destruction of art's *aura*, or the idea that a well-crafted, original object emanates its own power and energy that cannot be present in a reproduction, further inspired the hardening of art history's disciplinary boundary.

From this, art history grew to a field of study and knowledge production that privileged individual artists as creators and progressive historical chronologies. Some objects mattered more than others, according to art historical logic, and these objects formed a canon of great art. Visual analysis—the close looking at objects for form, technique, repetition, subject matter, symbol, and so on—was a crucial tool for unpacking meaning, defining style, and ascertaining both monetary and historical value. In other words, art history was a way of thinking about the massive and unruly world of visual objects by narrowing and bringing cohesion to chaos. This order came with the establishing of recognizable masterworks—a canon—that defined the art historical field. Works that had quality and meaning, that represented culture, style, and progress, would be valued for their ability to inspire intellectual and artistic progress. In a vast sea of objects and visual items, art history could give stability and narrative order—it was a port in the storm.

"Art" became a designation limited to the most important visual objects, identified as such by the experts: art historians. Art developed in a straight line from Giotto to Leonardo da Vinci, and from Leonardo to Diego Velázquez and to Jacques-Louis David, thence to Gustave Courbet, and from Courbet to Pablo Picasso and Jackson Pollock. A very straight, very male, and very white orderly line.

Thus, as art historian Kevin Moxey astutely notes, the art historian "often unwittingly engaged in the unthinking reproduction of culture: reproducing knowledge" and "as a consequence, the discipline as a whole becomes a powerful conservative force in a rapidly changing society."[22] The analysis, order, and styles that worked to unpack art became the very tools that hindered its growth. These conservative origins and the narrow canons they produced continue to shape and bedevil the field.

It was this sense of art history's limits, its inability to see past its own rules, its own canons, its own systems of value and meaning, that encouraged a rethinking of who and what mattered visually. Crucial to this shift was the growth and expansion of cultural studies in the 1960s and 1970s. As visual scholars Marita Sturken and Lisa Cartwright note, "one of the aims of cultural studies . . . was to provide viewers, citizens, and consumers with the tools to gain a better understanding of how we are produced as social subjects through the cultural practices that make up our lives."[23] Cultural studies scholars argued that the visual had always been a powerful tool for the transmission of ideas and values in any given community or society across time and space; the visual was a way to manifest the *cultural*. Their central issues and questions sought to determine how culture is made, what binds a given community together, what are its normative standards, how they are maintained, what happens when they are subverted or defied: in short, what stories societies tell in order to create the idea of themselves, and then how the visual reflects those narratives. Theorists such as Arjun Appadurai, Pierre Bourdieu, James Clifford, Stuart Hall, Mary Louise Pratt, and Raymond Williams reimagined the meanings of culture, particularly in relation to its foundations, definitions, and power, and the multiple ways individual subjects are policed, categorized, and able to navigate those power structures, and how they craft their identities. In this intellectual terrain, the visual is both a punitive and liberatory mechanism to embody, display, reflect, enact, and signify.

These theorists tend to deemphasize the object and the individual creativity or agency of its maker, suggesting that both are themselves socially constructed and specific; the what and the who of visual culture are incidental to its wider sociopolitical and cultural functions. Art, architecture, television, and all material objects reflect prior values and desires; they do not make them.

By the 1980s and early '90s, critical interventions of film theory, critical race theory, feminism, postcolonial studies, and queer theory added to the momentum of cultural studies' demands for an expansion of visual considerations from their art historical origins. The "gaze" and categories of race, gender, ability, and sexuality all grew as fundamental avenues to evaluate, interrogate, and expand or explode the canon. These critics and scholars asked *who* was defining beauty, *who* controlled the camera and what the camera was made to see, *who* was seen and *who* benefited from the canon and the category of "art" as contrasted with "non-art." There was a demand to critique and shift the power produced in knowledge, as well as the knowledge created by the powerful. In challenging notions of universalism, these scholars challenged the very definitions of perception and seeing.[24] If one judges the value, meanings, and utility of objects and images by narrow (read Western) cultural standards and situated norms, one misses the radical differences, the resistance to authority, and the terrible violence of visual claims to certain bodies. These scholars warned that previous ways of seeing had significant blinders, rendering so much and so many invisible.

Even terms such as "Renaissance" and "modernism" impose a chronology and sense of progression that is tied strictly to the "West" and empire, to the Enlightenment and colonial knowledge, excluding non-Western imagery, histories, and cultures. And this isn't only in the past; the terrible violence and skewed knowledge production continue, compounded in the oppressions, disparities, and global inequalities of our time.

By the 1990s and 2000s these new directions, interventions, and critiques had fundamentally shifted the parameters of the field of art history. Indeed, during this period some university and college departments shed the moniker "art history" altogether in favor of visual culture studies. This all suggests a growing awareness that visual culture represents a unique way of confronting the world and arranging and producing knowledge. The power of the "visual culture turn" has even impacted museums, locations that were fundamentally bound to the ideals, value schemas, and intellectual frameworks of art history. Widening the field of what constitutes "art" has allowed museums to do exhibitions on motorcycles, the television show

Downton Abbey, manga imagery, and the increasingly popular area of fashion and costume design. That the Metropolitan Museum of Art in New York hosts the annual Met Ball, in association with *Vogue* magazine, attracting the most elite celebrities of any given year, attests to what use visual culture has been to museum administrators desperate to expand audiences and get bodies into museum spaces. (More will be said in the next chapter about the idea of art and the history of the museum.)

Visual culture studies did not inaugurate these trends, but its development as a field and concept is inseparable from them. In this, our point of origin might be the first "blockbuster" museum exhibit and cultural phenomenon, "Treasures of Tutankhamun," more commonly known as the "King Tut exhibition," that opened at the Metropolitan Museum of Art in 1976. The show originated not from some specific interest in inspiring new dialogues about the aesthetic and formal values of Egyptian objects, but from political negotiations between President Richard Nixon, Secretary of State Henry Kissinger, and Egyptian President Anwar Sadat. It was not long before museums understood that the new emphasis on visual culture in scholarly circles would be helpful for broadening their audiences and missions in the late twentieth century. Thus, visual culture can be seen as a language for institutional rebranding and audience diversification.

In short, academically speaking, it was not one thing that created visual culture studies, but a series of shifts in knowledge, power, and authority that marked broad intellectual, political, and social changes in the last half of the twentieth century.

Yet this still doesn't tell us what visual culture is. The short answer: all of it. All of your visual memories, all of the images on screens, all of the objects in your house, everything in everyone else's house, all of the images on billboards, the sides of buses, and in subways, all the pictures of cities and farms, all the maps, all the cartoons, all the things you think you've seen but haven't yet. If you can see it, if it was made to be seen, then it's visual culture. But as Nicholas Mirzoeff advises, visual culture also "involves what is invisible or kept out of sight . . . we don't simply see what there is to see and call it visual culture. Rather we assemble a worldview that is consistent with what we know and have already experienced."[25] Or, as Sturken and Cartwright conclude, "we study visual culture and visuality in order to grasp their place in broader, multisensory networks of meaning and experience."[26] Visual culture is the study of everything in an attempt to understand it all. And just to be clear, participation in visual culture is not contingent on the ability to physically see. Those with visual impairments are swept into these dialogues of visual culture as part of the "multisensory networks." Physical sight is an element, but not the whole, of what visual culture is and does.

This is why visual *environment* is such a useful conceptualization. No visual object exists in isolation. Instead, when we see something, we are also seeing what is around it, what it reminds us of that came before, other memories of things we have seen or once heard of. And all these other shards of vision, all these fractured pieces of sight, collide into the experience, making it so that we can never see, and never look, in isolation. There is a past and a future to all present sights, and they exist simultaneously. Thus the urge to think about visual culture in clusters, environments, and constellations.

Even more useful might be thinking in terms of visual *atmospheres*. Atmospheres are tricky in that while they have definition and clear boundaries, these are not apparent in our day-to-day experience of them; we often cannot detect the contours until we have left the atmosphere. In other words, visual culture is always there but often unnoticed. It can seem natural, even organic, sustaining, and never-ending; it is like the air we breathe.

Until it is not. Until we have entered some other atmosphere where we are totally at a loss, where we can't breathe, where we are acutely and physically aware of a space that is denying us. While providing models of different meaning and effects, visual environments and visual atmospheres underscore the totalizing impact of the visual upon our lives, identities, and bodies, as well as naming our inability to fully define visual culture or ever escape its grasp.

This book uses the terms "image," "picture," "visual object," and "the visual" interchangeably, even though there are oceans of meaning among these words. This is not with the intent to confuse or to glory in imprecision—those differences matter.[27] But, for the purposes of our dialogue, and for the kinds of questions we need to ask about visual culture, I propose that we suspend tracking those differences here. We will consider the different categories of what gets called "art" or "popular," but you should always be mindful of the fact that those labels are themselves constructions rooted in history, relations of power, and situated in place and time. The same is true of the terms "image," "picture," and "object." They have histories, they have meant different things in different moments; a dress is not the same as a building, a painting is not a puppet, a commercial on television is not even a commercial on the internet. For our purposes, what visual culture *does* is more important than the boundaries of what it *is*.

In focusing on potential, on the breadth, instability, and ranging possibilities of visual culture, my hope is to remain open to thinking about how we know and see and how we might communicate in fresh ways, but also in fundamentally more inclusive, nimble, and empathic ways. Confronting visual culture and really studying it is a path to somewhere else, to a way of making different knowledge and new worlds. Scholar Kandice Chuh describes her somewhere else as "a space of encounters necessary to apprehending the world in uncommonsensical ways."[28] She urges pushing past the common wisdom, what is known and easy even when it's difficult, to the things that might balance the contradictions, reveal uncommon beauty or new angles, and show us new ways to be and relate. Visual culture can be understood, then, as the search for uncommonsensical worlds to inhabit and tend. What we have now might not be what you want, but it could be made—and seen—anew.

What potential?

While it is now cliché to say that a meme, image, or film "broke the internet," for a large population of people the internet was not just broken but quaking when Beyoncé and Jay-Z dropped the video for their 2018 single "Apeshit."[29] Depicting the celebrity power couple engaging the Western art canon and its many exclusions in the Louvre in Paris, the video went viral instantly and just as quickly generated dozens of think-pieces about art, race, power, and the ability to manipulate and even reinscribe museum spaces in the spirit of movements such as #blacklivesmatter and #decolonizethismuseum.[30] Reading lists, art history lessons, and crowdsourced syllabi proliferated. And every art history/visual culture major in the world finally felt some justification in their educational choices.

Yet, at the same moment, there were likely a very large group of viewers who did not understand what the fuss was about. It was a fairly typical music video, featuring the artists' undeniable style and gravitas, amazing clothes, and incredible dancers in an opulent setting. If you didn't know the space already or weren't looking very hard, you could miss that the video was filmed at the Louvre, one of the most famous and arguably most important museums in the world. If the viewer did not know the Louvre, what it looks like, what art is housed there, and perhaps even more importantly what art is *not* housed there, the video lost much of its radical power and racial rescripting.

Visual culture only has its full meaning if the context is clear, if the symbols reach the viewer. While you might have understood the moment Beyoncé and Jay-Z stand with the *Mona Lisa* between them as cool, if you did not realize they were really filming in the Louvre and the picture between was the real *Mona Lisa*, much of the impact of the visual was lost.

Thus, while there has been an enormous expansion of the field of visual culture, "knowing" is still the field's great anxiety. In the classroom, the most frequent phrase I hear, uttered in total frustration and despondency, is, "I just don't get it. Is there something I'm supposed to see here?" Visual culture seems implicated in this fear of not getting it, not seeing what you are supposed to, not being included: visual culture as #fomo. There is a whole genre of books that aims to teach audiences *how* to see: more creatively, more actively, with better perception. "Visual intelligence" is becoming its own self-help category, one that offers nothing short of "changing your life" and "art as therapy."[31]

Additionally, there is great anxiety in this particular historical moment about the changing conditions of visual culture: what it is, who controls it, how it is used to control us, who gets to study it, who makes money off it, what its boundaries are. We are repeatedly told that we live in the age of the visual, that we are overwhelmed with images and choices of images; almost weekly there are reports about how the visual and screens are shifting our cognitive abilities and destroying our perception and concentration. Yet what if this vexing "problem" of too much visual culture is not a problem at all? What if too many images and too many people talking about the visual are the heroic outcome, and not the declension, of the story?

This more optimistic and open version of visual culture has been articulated before. Mirzoeff, for example, suggests that in order to define "visual culture" we need to heed the questions more than the objects.[32] What he means here is that we need to not get so hung up on the thing, the art, or the image that we miss the bigger questions and problems, and thus the bigger story.

What happens when the visual pushes back against our stories? As noted earlier, images want things from audiences, and they can take them, aggressively and very often without consent. More and more neurological and psychological data suggests that people are powerless not to see and not to narrate what they see in ways that are externally triggered. Even this "data" is tied to previous ideas about perception and coercive capitalist imperatives. Can we even know what we want from images, or is all of this wanting predetermined for us?

Whichever way one turns, there is no clarity on the meaning and power and boundaries of visual culture. The desire to understand every image, to see it all clearly, to muster the cognitive control to override visual coercions is folly. Around all of us, images demand from audiences, they want audiences to commit. This commitment is complicated as it implicates audiences in vast systems and symbols that no one can fully grasp all of the time. It is impossible to know the origin story of each image, to know what every allusion refers to, to get the power dynamics in every representation. More important is to drill down to what the visual does to us and what we do to images.

This is to say even if you don't "know" who Beyoncé and Jay-Z are and why they are in the Louvre, we can start thinking about visual culture by asking why those particular images were made in a particular way, how the visuals collide with each other, what bodies are seen or made invisible, and what the relation is of the bodies to the images they stand next to. Finally, why are two people braiding their hair in what looks like a museum? Asking these questions gets us far closer to the meaning of the video than simply "knowing" could. These questions pull us to the urgent questions of visual culture: what is real, what is lasting, what do we deem precious, what are our obligations to see each other, can we ever understand the world around us and the spaces we share?

Artist/theorist Hito Steyerl pushes us to see the potential in this lack of fixity, in these big questions that demand big answers. She writes,

> The poor image is a copy in motion. Its quality is bad, its resolution substandard.... The poor image is no longer about the real thing—the originary original. Instead, it is about its own real conditions of existence: about swarm circulation, digital dispersion, fractured and flexible temporalities. It is about defiance and appropriation just as it is about conformism and exploitation. In short: it is about reality.[33]

Steyerl is speaking of repression and liberation, or a facet of "reality" as she terms it. Most of what we see is not "the real." Every representation in this book, for example, is a digital file manipulated and cut and resaved so many times that what we see is a mere phantom of the thing that we wish to represent or see. But to get hung up on this, to be distracted or dismayed, to talk down the image as having never really existed risks snobbery and misses the greater potential for liberation in the visual. We can never know the "real," so all we can play with is what we have. What we have, then, is visual culture. And that's where the potential lies.

In light of this, what exactly is Allahyari's *King Uthal*? In a visual culture sense, the object defies itself, its creator, and the audience. It quite literally does not exist in one place; the files for the production of the work can be infinitely shared, distributed, erased, each time fragmenting a bit as Steyerl wistfully promised. Can the viewer depend on this object, or is the work instead always trying to slip away from everyone's grasp? The piece hangs, in other words, between creation and destruction.

In considering Allahyari's *King Uthal* as visual culture we need to *see* this object in radically different ways, contradictory ways. It is a piece of plastic that pulls at time and art and memory and violence in dozens of ways. And in fact, what is it that you the reader see here? Do you see just the object, in its space, or do you think of the original *King Uthal*? Are you also thinking about the other versions that exist of Allahyari's work, and where those pieces might be? Or is the clarity of the plastic reminding you of ice sculptures and cheap plastic silverware, disappearing and disposable as perhaps this work is?

All the answers are valid, and important. The artist asks us to think of the object not in isolation but in a kind

Visual culture is hard and messy business. It always has been. Images want to tussle.

of atmosphere, of blueprints and documents and JPEGs and of a time here but also a time long ago. There is also violence all around this image, because of course we are reminded of the desire to silence the visual, to shut it up, to control it. But we are reminded also of the visual's refusal to be silenced, shut up, controlled.

Visual culture is never singular or static. Images circulate and change in an environment of probable meanings and possible outcomes that are not infinite, but at the same time are never entirely closed off to outside influence. Visual culture is without hard boundaries and temporally fluid, merging past, present and future. It is overwhelmingly vast and slips easily through your fingers, but we can consider elements within a myriad of currents, cross-currents, and episodic bursts.

Visual culture is hard and messy business. It always has been. Images want to tussle. We must think harder and smarter about tussling back. For every ancient handprint we see on a cave wall, we must ask, whose hand did not warrant an outline? For every historic site we look at in wonder, we must also whisper to ourselves, why was this preserved and not that? What was destroyed or torn down to build this? We always need to look closely and ask, why this and not . . . well, anything else? What do we want, and how are we left wanting?

2

WHERE

The entire world is shining with things we cannot see.
Akiko Busch[1]

Provocation

It was meant to be a grand reopening and celebration of the successful partnership between the Walker Art Center and the Minneapolis Park and Recreation Board in the Minneapolis Sculpture Garden featuring public works from the Walker's collection. The event would also see the unveiling of eighteen sculptures new to the collection, including a work by Sam Durant called *Scaffold*. On May 25, 2017, the Walker's executive director, Olga Viso, distributed a release promoting the public opening, which was scheduled for June 3.[2] In it, she celebrated the upcoming event as marking the successful culmination of a multi-year, multimillion-dollar renovation of the Garden, and referenced Durant's new work.

The public/private collaboration that created the Garden in 1988 offered a range of benefits to the Walker Art Center. The public space for quiet repose and engagement with art in central Minneapolis would come to include over 60 works, many of them site-specific. This partnership with the city worked to cement the Walker Art Center's place as a valued community institution in Minneapolis and in Minnesota at large, as well as a contemporary art

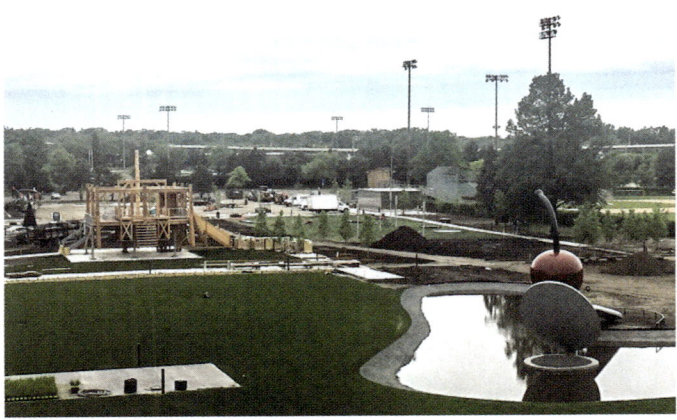

Figure 4 A view of the Minneapolis Sculpture Garden with Claes Oldenburg and Coosje van Bruggen's *Spoonbridge and Cherry* at right and Sam Durant's *Scaffold* at left. Photo: Sheila Regan/Hyperallergic.

destination for national and international audiences. This facet of the relationship was all the more important given the Walker's unusual exclusive focus on contemporary art and its embrace of exhibitions and installations that are visually and often politically provocative.

Sculptor Sam Durant's was a familiar name to the Walker, as he had had a residency there when still an emerging artist in 2002. Ten years later, he was an established figure known for his political works addressing the violent racial and economic histories of the United States. *Scaffold* was a work he had originally made for documenta 13, in Kassel, Germany, in 2012. A prestigious exhibition with an august reputation, documenta is held every five years and eschews sales, reinforcing its reputation for showcasing new talents and the interesting rather than the merely marketable. Artists are chosen to participate and then given two years to prepare their works for exhibition. The Walker, no doubt encouraged by Durant's successful career following his residency and the pedigree of this specific piece, purchased *Scaffold* in 2014. The inclusion of the piece in the reopened Garden was meant to celebrate its addition to the Walker's permanent collection.

Scaffold is a recreation of gallows used by the United States for state-ordered executions between 1859 and 2006 at various federal installations within and beyond the nation's borders. Made of wood and steel, the work is described thus by Durant:

The reconstructed gallows are built on top of and
into each other to form a single, integrated unit . . .
around a center point . . . so that the deck of the
most recent gallows forms the bottom layer with
each successive layer built up chronologically. The
viewer can explore the structural aspects underneath
the deck while children have ready-made climbing
frames. Visitors can then access the platform via
two staircases where factual information about the
project can be found.[3]

In her statement to the museum community and public, Viso provided the broad historical and political context for the piece, including site-specific Minnesota connections:

Of the seven gallows depicted in Durant's sculpture,
there is one specific to Minnesota history: the
gallows design related to the execution of the Dakota
38 in Mankato, Minnesota in 1862. The Mankato
Massacre represents the largest mass execution in
the history of the United States, in which 38 Dakota
men were executed by order of President Lincoln in
the same week that the Emancipation Proclamation
was signed. It is one of the greatest atrocities in
the history of our state and in the history of capital
punishment. The artist has referenced this event
along with the other six scaffolds that comprise

the structure, which include those used to execute abolitionist John Brown (1859); the Lincoln Conspirators (1865), which included the first woman executed in US history; the Haymarket Martyrs (1886), which followed a labor uprising and bombing in Chicago; Rainey Bethea (1936), the last legally conducted public execution in US history; Billy Bailey (1996), the last execution by hanging (not public) in the US; and Saddam Hussein (2006), for war crimes at a joint Iraqi/US facility.[4]

Durant was clear that his piece was to be understood as an examination of racist and genocidal US policies over time, as well as a reflection on the contemporary death penalty, mass incarceration, and the carceral state. He noted, "We now know that one in one hundred U.S. citizens are in jail and one in nine African American men are in prison. . . . We know that innocent people have been executed and that there are many potentially innocent prisoners sitting on death row today. It is to this context that *Scaffold* is addressed."[5]

According to the artist and the Walker, *Scaffold* was intended to engage the public in dialogues about history, memory, race, federal punishment, and corporeality. Its value to these dialogues was authorized by Durant's history with the Walker, his subsequent success, the piece's origins in documenta, and many positive reviews.

Presumably *Scaffold*'s specific value to the Garden and the people of Minneapolis was in its ability to engage these thorny issues while serving the multigenerational needs of a community park. In the eyes of the museum and Durant, it seemed a perfect fit.

Yet, less than twenty-four hours after the Walker's online statement, protesters were picketing at the Garden and a #takeitdown social media campaign was rocketing around Twitter. Indigenous activists and their allies had four immediate objections to *Scaffold*: (1) even though the main reference at the center of the sculpture was the murder of 38 Dakota in Minnesota, no Dakota elders or other tribal representatives from the state were consulted about the work or about locating the piece in the Garden; (2) museum officials and Durant had ignored or not considered the sculpture's great potential to (re)traumatize Indigenous visitors to the park and to wider communities beyond it; (3) the work was created by a non-Indigenous artist whose choice to aggregate so many different executions over such a wide span of time diminished the specificity of each, and this reinforced the disappearing of Indigenous subjects, alive and dead; and (4) the location of the sculpture among several whimsical public works and the express encouragement of children to play and climb on it was deeply inappropriate to the subject matter, another act of careless disrespect for the traumatic collective and personal histories of Minnesota's Indigenous people.

Word of the protest spread on social media and was quickly picked up by local news outlets. Caught off-guard, the museum and Durant responded in haste to the angry charges of the protesters. Viso issued a public apology on behalf of the Walker Art Center, noting that she regretted not reaching out to Indigenous communities in the city and state before and was sorry "that [she] did not better anticipate how the work would be received in Minnesota, especially by Native audiences." Apologizing "for any pain and disappointment that the sculpture might elicit," the museum's director concluded with her intent to reach out now to local representatives, particularly those from Indigenous communities, so they might begin a more productive dialogue.[6]

The letter only further inflamed the protestors and critics. With the promise of more protests to come, Viso issued a second statement reporting that the sculpture would be removed.[7] The decision was made, Viso noted, in consultation with Durant who reasoned, "It's just wood and metal—nothing compared to the lives and histories of the Dakota people."[8] The statement added that all further discussions about the sculpture's "dismantling would happen in consultation with the Dakota tribe." The time from Viso's initial celebratory promotion of the Garden's reopening to the statement that Durant's *Scaffold* would be removed from the park was one week.

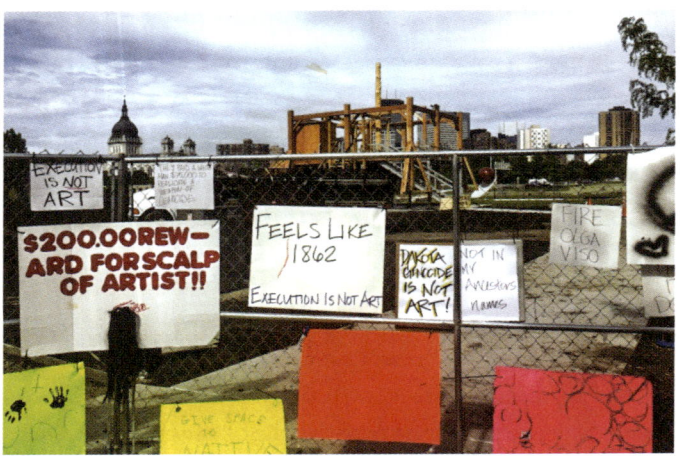

Figure 5 Protest signs on the fence near Sam Durant's *Scaffold* in the Minneapolis Sculpture Garden. Sheila Regan/Hyperallergic.

After numerous meetings, the Garden's installation of *Scaffold* was dismantled and given to the Dakota Tribe. A few months later the Walker created its first Indigenous Art Committee tasked with commissioning a new sculpture for the Garden by an Indigenous artist. The Walker still technically owns *Scaffold*, as each iteration of the work was made by Durant to be site-specific—the work was removed from public space, but not decommissioned by the museum.

Viso stepped down from her position as executive director a few months after the *Scaffold* incident. While the press noted that it did not appear that she had been fired, the timing was suspicious. Commenting on Viso's departure, Glenn Lowry, director of the Museum of Modern Art in New York, seemed to commiserate about how hard it was to run a museum in the current environment. "People are agitated," he said, "and communities that have felt disadvantaged or marginalized are particularly agitated because they feel vulnerable, and rightly so."[9]

Reporter and activist Ashley Fairbanks's reaction to the controversy was a bit different: "White artist. Dakota pain. Dakota Genocide. White entertainment. . . . I've grown so tired of white people stealing our joy and our time and our energy and not understanding our rage."[10]

Where can I find it?

This chapter examines the importance of location, geographies of meaning, and mobility—the *where* of visual culture. This is often represented through a binary of inside and outside. Being on the inside means approval, status, and space. Outside, conversely, suggests something too wild, too awful, too mundane, or too dangerous to be allowed in. Inside is art, respect, money, historical meaning, value, power, and things craved; outside is kitsch, popular culture, craft, advertising, trash, fluff, historical oblivion, and the unwanted.

The question of where also pulls us back to the visual environment and the visual atmosphere. *Where* an object is seen, where it is visible, attaches itself to the object. Objects are changed when they are moved into new environments; new ecosystems can add or subtract value, so that new surroundings alter meanings. A visual atmosphere can also nurture an image, performance, or object, giving it life and a place to breathe. But whereas one atmosphere can animate certain visual imagery, this same atmosphere can suffocate others, making something once vibrant inert. Where we see things, what location we identify them with, works to shape visual culture. Where also highlights how changeable the visual is, how ideas about meaning morph depending on location.

Inside and outside likewise come with baggage. Inside seems cozy and well-tended, but it can also be boring, normal, safe, and stifling. Great power can be found outside. There is freedom in the outside, as well as authenticity, righteousness, and alternative forms of belonging. There is power in invisibility, in flying under the radar, in staying unseen. Outside—cast off the metaphorical island—is where many want their visual culture to remain.

This all points to the limited usefulness and endemic obfuscations of binary categories such as "inside/outside." A more apt metaphor for visual culture might be a vortex. Everything gets pulled in and swirled together in a vortex, and there is always the possibility—even the probability—of being simply overwhelmed, mixed up, and dragged under and out of sight.

It is also crucial to keep in mind in this chapter *where* you are in visual culture. Where do you go to see things? Where do you go to be seen? Where are you allowed to look or prohibited from looking? The geography of visual culture is not just about objects but also about audience. Technology also shifts the dialogue of inside and outside, making where all the more fundamental to visual culture.

Get Inside

Conceding the profound limitations of binary explanations, we can still say that art is squarely on the inside. Right?

Today, few would disagree that Judy Chicago's *The Dinner Party* (1974–1979) was a groundbreaking political, artistic, and public event. When the piece was first shown in 1979 at the San Francisco Museum of Art, over 100,000 people went to look at it. It is a massive work, and contains not even a moment of visual silence. Each table in the triangle is 48 feet long and everything, from every plate and napkin to the tablecloth and even the tiles on the floor, has some kind of writing, imagery, and messaging. Articles and outrage followed the opening, but it was clear that this work, and all of its prominent racial and

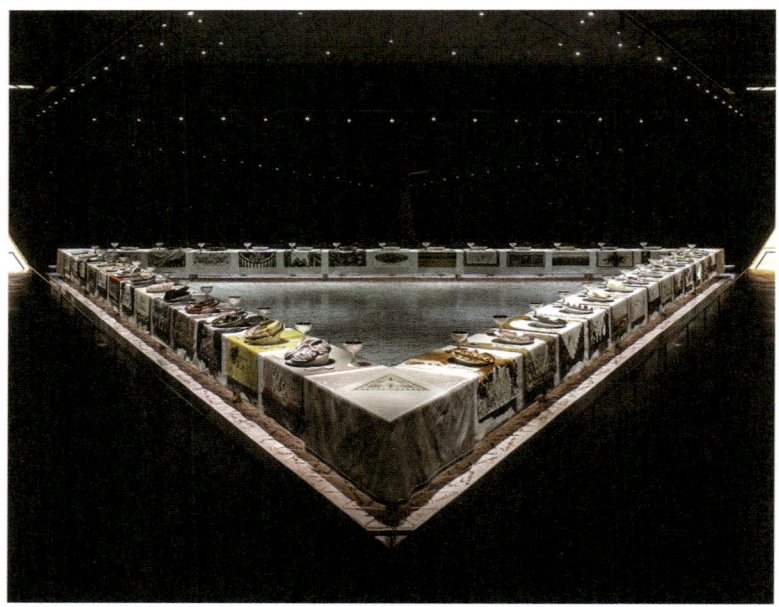

Figure 6 Judy Chicago, *The Dinner Party*, 1979. Mixed media, 36 × 576 × 576 in. Installed in its permanent home at the Elizabeth A. Sackler Center for Feminist Art at the Brooklyn Museum, Brooklyn, New York. © Judy Chicago / Artists Rights Society (ARS), New York. Photo: © Donald Woodman / ARS, NY.

representational problems, mattered to a great number of people who were deeply engaged with thinking and writing about art and society.

Sounds like something that should have been in a museum, doesn't it?

For more than two decades, it wasn't. Until 2002, *The Dinner Party* spent most of its time packed up in crates and in storage. Despite the years spent by the artist and others trying to find a home for it, no major (or minor) art institution would purchase the work; nor could a donor be convinced to gift it to a museum. During this time, it was written about in almost every scholarly and general account of American feminism and feminist art, it was noted in histories of material culture, it was a common reference to explain political art, and it was regularly taught in art history and women's studies classrooms. Yet it could not be seen as it was created or as the artist intended. All those scholars, readers, activists, and students had were some washed-out pictures.

Without the imprimatur of a museum or other art institution, Chicago's work had a tenuous claim to the label "art," which in turn further distanced it from the realm of possibility for collections and limited acquisition budgets. And while some called it "art," many others saw the work as nothing more than feminist "propaganda," or as mere "kitsch," "craft," or the vague "popular." It might be many things, but it was not art.[11] This dismissal was itself profoundly gendered, sequestering *The Dinner Party* and its considerations to the realms of women and defining those realms as distinct from and less representative than major works and artists.

This changed in 2002, when the Brooklyn Museum of Art in New York was given the piece by Elizabeth A. Sackler.[12] In 2007, the museum opened the Elizabeth A. Sackler Center for Feminist Art, the first of its kind at a nonacademic institution, with *The Dinner Party* as its centerpiece, pun intended. Judy Chicago and her work had, as it were, finally been invited to the party. It was a belated victory for Chicago and feminist art, and a win for the Brooklyn Museum. Inside, at last.

It does matter where an object lands. Power, memory, value all come into play with the where of visual culture, because this involves questions of what is worth seeing and who gets to decide. The question of what is made available to see and in which locations—what is inside the frame and what is cast out—has been fundamental to all considerations of visual culture. The very notion of "art," for example, is predicated on a core belief that some things are visually better than others and that some people have special gifts (genius) in making these things. By attributing greater value to these people and their creations, the terms "artist" and "art" take on greater representational meaning and cultural authority; they become the measure of beauty, craft, talent, and human progress. The art historian Michael Kelley describes this elevating transmutation from thing and situation to art like this: "What is transfigured here is thus not the images per se but their meanings, which are *taken out of history* and *taken up into art*."[13] To be taken up into art changes the where. Art is cared for, valued, remembered, and seen.

With Judy Chicago's *The Dinner Party* we can see this recategorization at work. *The Dinner Party* was always important to its historical moment and became a critical part of the historical dialogue. To many it was *always* art. It was really only settled within the category of art, however, when it was installed at the Brooklyn Museum. The work was transformed. Location, location, location.

It is important to remember that the idea of art is not transhistorical or global. As we briefly touched on in chapter 1, "art" grew in Western Europe as cultural construct alongside ideas such as the nation-state, capitalism, and individuality. From these nurturing agents "art" was an idea theorized and normalized and given a history and a logic in written texts; it was displayed in public and private spaces dedicated to showing "art;" it was made precious by activating adjacent terms such as time, monetary value, and scarcity; it was given social and spiritual powers to make society better or worse; its makers were deemed "artists" and then occasionally promoted to geniuses.

Part of the functional definition of art also became that, from a European perspective, the rest of the world was not

The very notion of "art" is predicated on a core belief that some things are visually better than others and that some people have special gifts (genius) in making these things.

making "real" art. There were objects of value, utility, and ceremony, and there was clear importance and meaning in visual codes and communication. Other cultures might even think they made something that was art. But none of this was art of the same caliber as that made in the West. This claim of art's absence outside the West came to symbolize a lack of progress and human refinement, and was thus foundational to the development of Western hierarchies of civilization, race, and self-possession. This, in turn, rationalized and fueled empire, slavery, and the violent extraction of resources—people who did not make objects of art could themselves be made into objects. The where of art has a very bloodied history.[14]

Again, this did not mean that objects from non-Western locations did not have value. Beauty and power were often assigned to non-Western objects through their categorization as "folk," "naive," "primitive," "exotic," "mysterious," "simplistic," "authentic." These words, however, all coded outsiderness, signaling that their acceptance was always with a caveat, a "neat, but not great, not genius, not art—just different." Which is why for so many artists and individuals, being put in a museum, having their ancestors' work called "art" and studied in this very narrow lane, is not a compliment but an insult and a form of violence. While some populations view art as a designation of respect, of value, of honor, for others this designation is nothing more than another oppressive idea, part of the larger power dynamics of colonialism, cultural genocide, and disrespect.

The Indigenous peoples of the area that is now the southeast coast of Alaska had lived through the ebb and flow of empires, conquest, disease, and warfare long before 1867 when their land was purchased from Russia by the US federal government. Long before, and long after, the people of the Pacific Northwest made totem poles, although these poles were known by other names, Gyáa'aang for example to the Haida peoples. It was not just the name that changed, but the very value and meaning of these poles. American and European collectors who were predominantly white began to see Tlingit and Haida totem poles as objects of skilled craftsmanship and beauty, as things worth viewing from places belonging to *them* or under their stewardship. They removed them from their original locations, which were remote from the vast majority of white Americans and Western Europeans, and relocated them to parks and museums where the public, *their* publics, could see them.

Where the poles stood is in fact fundamental to their intended function. The poles' specificities of meaning, community, and ceremony relied on their locations and relationships to the people for whom they were originally made. They carried tribal stories and histories, but their intentions varied. For individual Tlingit and Haida communities, totem poles could serve as memorials and

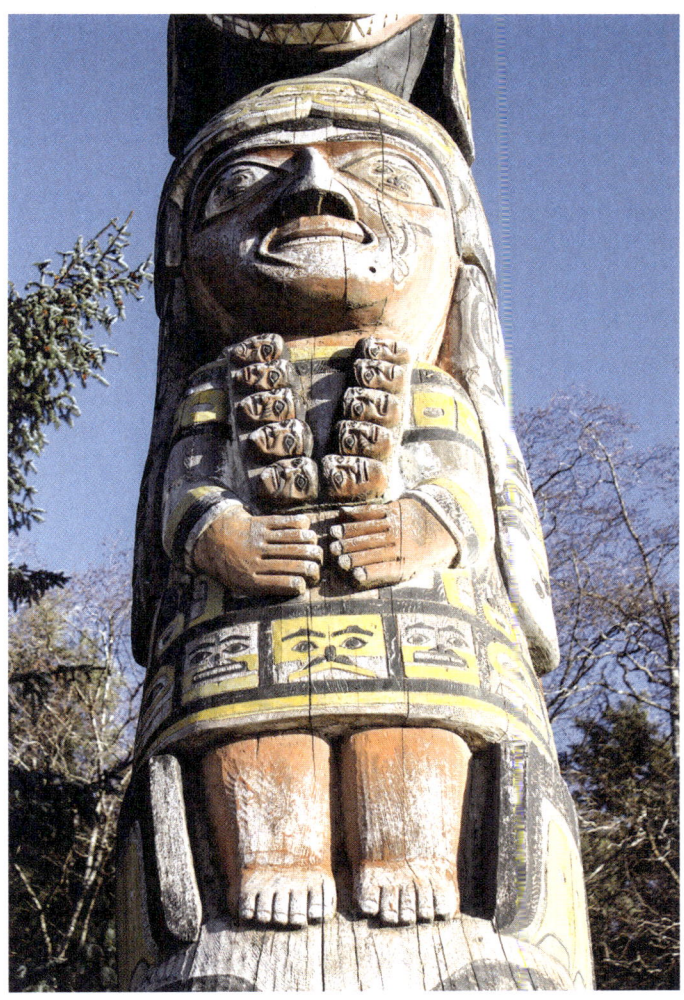

Figure 7 Detail of the Master Carver pole by John Wallace at Totem Bight State Historical Park, near Ketchikan, Alaska. Pole completed in 1941. Photo by permission from Emily Moore.

markers of honor, or broadcast shame and ridicule. Meaning depended on site and location.[15] All the meaning of place, however, was of little concern when the poles that had stood for generations in specific locations were taken and essentially replanted: a violence in some ways doubly rendered, first in stripping the Indigenous peoples of their works and second in displaying them in new and unfamiliar contexts.

Uprooted and relocated to personal collections and museums, the poles were given new meaning in their new locations. Nontribal connoisseurs, scholars, and collectors imbued the poles with new values and aesthetic importance as "art" and "historical artifacts." The poles were made to tell new stories of civilization, imperial authority, and cosmopolitanism. The objects themselves, what they looked like and their properties, were unchanged, yet their meaning had changed.

From one perspective, the reclassification of totem poles as art, as worthy, as valid and interesting enough to be in places that are structured to highlight looking, meant inclusion and diversity and expanding the visual picture. Indeed, in newer, more heavily trafficked locations the poles would be seen more, and thus the skills, history, and talents of the tribes that made them would have more purchase in a different visual context. Yet from another perspective, this movement and this new identity were merely another insult, another disappearance, another expansionist, colonialist vision that robbed the people of their story.

Therein lies the rub, or rather bludgeon, of visual culture. Names, categories, definitions, ownership, and the authority to tell a history all have powerful, transformative, often brutal effects. Moving a Tlingit totem pole or *The Dinner Party* to a museum space doesn't change the object itself, nor does securing these objects' categorizations as types of "art," and yet the relocations change the objects. A change of where shifts the visual environment and makes for new meanings.

As to museums: although they began in a particular place and in a particular time dedicated to a specific version of art, museums are now major international sites of political, cultural, and visual exchange.[16] To be blunt, they are places that house visual objects that have been deemed worthy of being seen. Some objects are in, some are out. But thinking about the museum as a storehouse of what audiences are *allowed and encouraged* to see gives some sense of what it then means to be both inside and outside these kinds of spaces.

"Museum," importantly, is shorthand for a whole range of public and private places dedicated to qualifying, organizing, and creating knowledge about objects. World's fairs, galleries, parks, zoos, salons, and spaces like freak shows, starting in the sixteenth century and morphing into twentieth-century circuses, are all museum-adjacent, or have a shared DNA. They are all spaces created to teach people how to look, what to look at, and certain things they are supposed to know about what they have seen. These spaces are rooted in the idea of taking objects (animals, people, vases, etc.) from one location or a "natural" environment and placing them in a context which is (1) totally structured around the act of looking, (2) a deeply controlled environment, and (3) focused on communicating certain contained ideas about the meaning of the object in this new space. Sound a bit manipulative? Nothing about these spaces is random or benign. Looking and knowing are the point, and each of us is led from point A to point B.

Which is why, as scholar Svetlana Alpers cheekily notes, "museums can make it hard to see."[17] These spaces all promote the idea of access, of the liberty to come someplace and see something with your own eyes. The idea of audience individuality is always being sold, as theoretically the audience is judge and jury. Objects are put out in the open to be consumed, and this suggests a kind of democracy of exchange of ideas.

Yet the objects have all been chosen, they have been arranged, identified, and categorized. Mammals in zoos don't go with reptiles, Netherlandish fourteenth-century painting is never mixed in with Indonesian shadow puppets. Or consider all the museums at Harvard University, from the Peabody Museum of Archaeology and Ethnology to the Natural History Museum to the art museums.

As visual theorists David Carrier and Joachim Pissarro ask, "What, exactly, are the distinctions . . . that house multitudes of objects and histories?"[18] These distinctions follow and replicate logics and knowledges about culture; in other words, they tell the story Harvard, or the Louvre, or Barnum and Bailey, or various national governments want told. The space, the inside, then communicates value and how we are allowed to see things. Where in a museum an object goes means everything about how audiences will see it, understand it, and value it. How indeed could we ever "see" in a museum? All the objects have already been seen for us, and thus we are less seeing than being fed stories.

Visual culture theorist Tony Bennett goes in for the kill: "Museums . . . were to arrange their displays so as to simulate the organization of the world—human and natural—outside museum walls."[19] The inside, thus, is always and already about manipulating the understanding of the outside. The museum, and all these locations of display, move with an agenda. Ever wonder why there is no African art in the Louvre? (Beyoncé sure did.) Wonder why Islamic art was let in and African art had to be placed in other buildings? Inside and outside are never random.[20]

How many times does the object shift meaning in arriving at a museum display? Objects are first chosen to be in these spaces. They are then isolated in there, cut off from any other occasion or situation they might have had (even contemporary art, much of which is made with the understanding that it will end up in a museum, has been detoured from other temporal and physical realities by being placed there). They are placed in spaces with other objects that it has been decided they have kinship with. Finally, they are given tags, titles, identities that provide further context outside of the visual. Each of these stages makes the object perhaps harder and harder to see, as the messaging of the space becomes more and more heavily managed.

Inside, therefore, might grant objects less acceptance, power, and control than might first appear. For each object that makes it inside becomes beholden to another agenda, and in some sense loses, perhaps permanently, its chance to be anything else visually and culturally. In noting that museums make it hard to see, Alpers was suggesting that this fog, this distortion has real costs. If *The Dinner Party* established one kind of stability in entering the Brooklyn Museum, it also lost other possibilities. Coming inside also means that *The Dinner Party* visually is owned by the Brooklyn Museum, which now controls some of the rights to the piece and can decide (to a certain extent) where the work can be viewed and by whom. More nefariously, a museum can always decide *not* to exhibit a work: to put it in storage or move it offsite where it is effectively hidden. Value and visibility are at the discretion of an institution with its own agenda.

Inside, however, can be a place of visual resistance as well. Returning to the example Tlingit and Haida totem poles, another story about authority emerges. While many totems were removed under problematic circumstances, inadvertently space arose for a new dialogue with indigenous populations. As art historian Emily L. Moore argues, New Deal federal funding programs wanted public parks to represent new inclusive versions of what American looked like. As part of this larger program, it was decided that it was crucial to repair and reinstall totem poles in public parks. It would be easy to see this as yet another moment when the object and its meanings for a community were visually hijacked, repurposed and lost to the original makers. Yet, as Moore suggests, Tlingit and Haida used this moment to assert their own skills, their own contemporary visual narratives, and even more importantly their claims to sovereignty.[21] If meaning can be reassigned, then perhaps it can be reassigned in ways that benefit those seeking to make claims on power and space.

The reach of museums and affiliated spaces in regard to the future of visual culture is only expanding. Art centers and museums have grown as economic and tourist anchors, and numerous museums, such as the Louvre and the Guggenheim, have expanded their "brand" with international satellites. Museums might also seem like physical locations, but they have been aggressively moving into the digital sphere. Collections of most major museums are available on their websites, and major museums are now allowing their images to be downloaded and published without cost. This means their names and their art get written about more and seen more. Museums also encourage patrons to Instagram their spaces and events and give daily awards for the best postings. Cameras and reproductions used to be carefully monitored and restricted, but the internet and social media have moved the visual atmosphere of the museum into this new virtual space. Museums have learned to play with new technology, and they have used it to move their images, their ideas about art, their power and status as visual cultural authorities to new audiences and new generations.[22] A museum's where is starting to be everywhere.

Inside, therefore, continues to expand. As noted in the last chapter, the power of museums and visual culture was demonstrated and reinforced by the "Apeshit" video of Beyoncé and Jay-Z. The video brought the Louvre to new audiences, and even though the video aggressively engaged the very difficult and deeply racist history of that (and of all) museums in regard to non-white bodies, the video, by featuring the Louvre, could not help reinvesting in the authority of the Louvre specifically, and of museums generally, as the most important, most prestigious, and most inside of visual culture locations. Beyoncé and Jay-Z took the fight to the Louvre, and the Louvre administration—no doubt sensing the opportunity

Museums have learned to play with new technology, and they have used it to move their images, their ideas about art, their power and status as visual cultural authorities to new audiences and new generations.

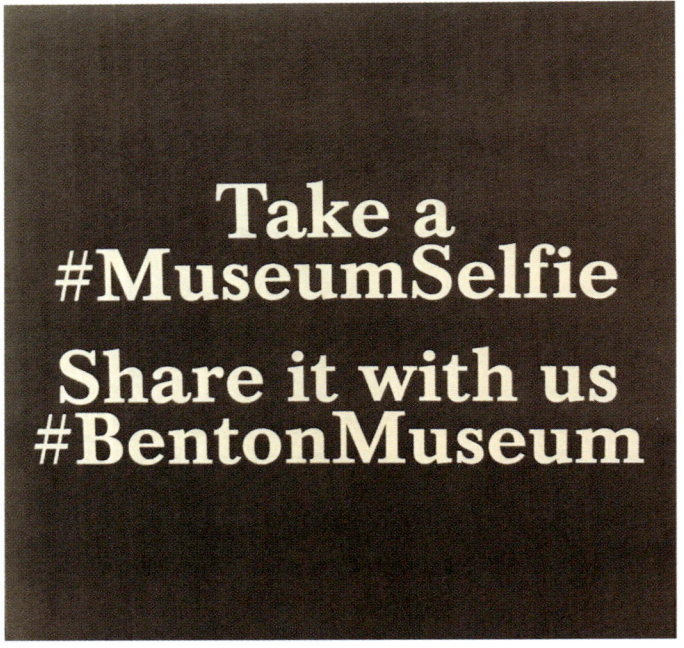

Figure 8 Sign at the William Benton Museum of Art, Storrs, Connecticut. Photo by author with permission from the Benton Museum.

to grab more eyes, to be seen even more, to grow their where—gave permission to film.

This cycle of insider visibility was expanded again when Beyoncé and Jay-Z won the 2019 BRIT award for Best International Group. The couple did not make the ceremony but instead sent a short video acceptance reprising a moment from their "Apeshit" video where the two stand frontally facing the camera in sharp clothes. In the "Apeshit" video the painting between the couple is Leonardo's *Mona Lisa*, the most famous work of art, famously coveted and housed at the Louvre behind inches of bulletproof glass. The moment from the original video is a moment of power and access, for it is widely known that to see the *Mona Lisa* regular people have to stand behind hordes of other visitors and patiently wait to be jostled up to the front to get a close look at the painting. Why does everyone wait? Because it is the most famous painting in the world. Why? The *Mona Lisa*'s fame and importance are in some ways beyond self-evident. They just are. Thus, when Beyoncé and Jay-Z stand next to this most famous, most important, most valued painting of a white woman, they are visually reframing her fame with theirs. Just as her fame and importance and meaning are self-evident, so are theirs. It is the ultimate visual power move. Three equals in perfection, importance, power. Three on the inside. Race is also engaged in this visual, with Beyoncé and Jay-Z also powerfully noting, in this one moment of this one video, that the mantle of beauty and power, historically preserved and replicated in the Louvre as that of white bodies, has been extended. Here, two black bodies flank the *Mona Lisa*, making her the odd white lady out.

In the BRIT awards video, however, it is quickly apparent that they are not in the Louvre, because the painting

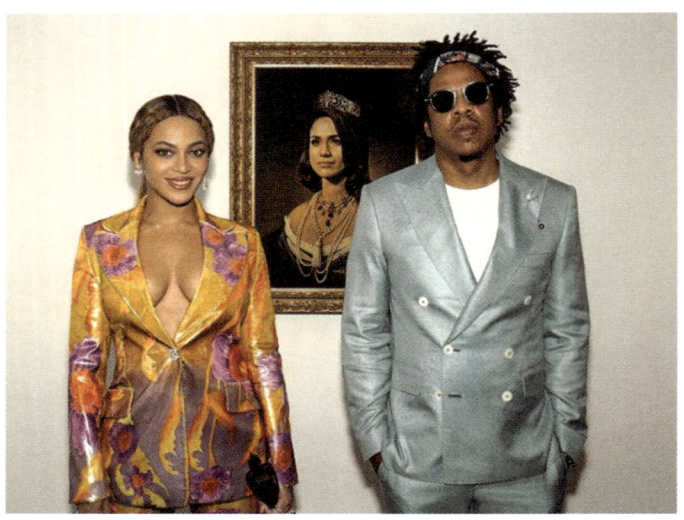

Figure 9 Beyoncé and Jay-Z, screen shot of Instagram, February 20, 2019. https://www.instagram.com/p/BuHvVDPgVdF/?utm_source=ig_embed.

between them is not the *Mona Lisa* but a portrait of Meghan Markle, the Duchess of Sussex. Markle, an American biracial actress, blogger, and activist, famously and with no shortage of controversy had married Prince Harry, Duke of Sussex, and at the time of the video was pregnant with the couple's first child. Marrying into the British royal family was already enough to keep the notoriously aggressive tabloids very busy, but Markle also became a target of racist imagery and commentary. To phrase it another way, the press was consistently looking for ways to highlight that Markle was outside to the royalty, not inside. This point was then cruelly and publicly made by Princess Michael of Kent, who, attending a family event where Megan and Harry were present, wore a blackamoor pin. Blackamoor is the decorative use of a dark black figure in jewelry or housewares, associated with colonial, racist histories by reducing the black body to a generic decorative flourish. This small piece of jewelry served as a reminder about which bodies had meaning, and which could be made small and insignificant.

This was precisely the dialogue about race, but also about inside and outside, that Beyoncé and Jay-Z clearly sought to disrupt. The placing of the portrait of Markle where the *Mona Lisa* had stood in the previous video was clearly a message; there was a new version of royalty, beauty, and art in town, and it was Markle. Whiteness had been moved out of the frame altogether, and three powerful, successful, proud, political black Americans stood, accepting the British prizes they had won. Thus, Markle was inside the circle of blackness and power. Markle is also positioned and dressed not in her contemporary clothes, but in high regal garb, looking more like a queen than a duchess. And this too was an inside allusion, as Beyoncé is typically referred to by her fans as Queen Bey. All hail the queens.

The where of inside moves. It can be an idea of value and worth, it can be called art and used to make things precious and also weaponized to legitimate and sustain power and ideology. It can be in museums, but these locations that began as strictly physical locations constructed to house art and aura and originality have morphed to move across the internet, onto Instagram feeds and Twitter timelines. The power of these visual warehouses, to create an inside that can grow but always maintains an exclusivity, stays constant.

It is easy to dismiss both art and museums as old-school visual culture, as warehouses of yesterday's ideas and theories about what can be seen and what can't. But if people still covet, and technology still enables, an entry inside, then it is unwise to imagine that museums' power and authority have shifted too radically. Ultimately, *The Dinner Party* was always going to end up in a museum, if only to prove how museum spaces shift and change. Ultimately, too, we will see Beyoncé's and Jay-Z's clothes, props, and videos move into museum spaces. These locations are where visual and cultural power resides. There is power on the inside.

But perhaps that case shouldn't be oversold just yet.

Get Out

Thomas Kinkade is the most owned artist in the world. This is technically hard to verify, but if the measure is how many products have been bought with his imagery on them, it is difficult to think of a counterexample. The *Mona Lisa* or even Beyoncé might be more visually recognizable, and likely most people could not summon up any of Kinkade's specific titles or images. Regardless, his soft, impressionist-styled, semireligious, landscape-meets-Walt Disney aesthetic reportedly featured in one in twenty homes in the United States in the 1990s and 2000s.[23]

Yet original Kinkade paintings are still not owned by any major American museum. Kinkade himself seemed to understand that being an outsider was to be his true contribution to the dialogue of visual culture. He repeatedly sought to prove, once and for all, the total shell game that was the idea of the art world and its constructed notions of value, quality, and worth. His visual images spoke to millions; even more than a decade after his death, his company still produces new images, circulates new merchandise, and shows no signs of losing its appeal to a large audience.

The accusation most typically thrown at Kinkade's imagery was that it was not in fact art but kitsch. This label has been used for most of the past century as a mechanism of exclusion and derision, most sharply by the critic Clement Greenberg, who began writing in the buildup to World War II and then established himself as an advocate for postwar abstract expressionism. To Greenberg, kitsch described how a visual object, in its banality, its easiness, its slipperiness, could manage to seduce the masses into looking, staring, and consuming.[24] For Greenberg, kitsch wasn't exactly a visual quality. It was instead the way a constellation of visual qualities manipulated the viewer. Too much kitsch was like too much candy; it would make the world sick and incapable of liberating itself from injustice. Only art could ultimately motivate and inspire people to overcome the bonds of injustice and misunderstanding that separated them. Art could heal, and it would heal through provocation, through moving culture forward. In this sense, Greenberg was insisting on the category of art as something morally instructive and inspirational. Kitsch, on the other hand, meant withdrawal, distraction, a lack of agency for the viewer. In Greenberg's terms, kitsch was essentially an evil.

Kitsch does not always carry such intensive moral implications, but it has become a shorthand for a kind of cultural meaninglessness. Something that is kitsch can summon intense and positive feelings, but those feelings are not deemed authentic or real. Alienating the viewer from the epic and intense, kitsch is seen to play on weaknesses, evoking feelings that are performative and fake.

Thus, for those who see Kinkade as kitsch, his images do not provoke the viewer or push them to see something anew. They are passive, unoriginal, uninspiring. They keep the viewer stuck. Does it matter that millions of people disagree, that they purchase Kinkade's work and bring it into their homes? A Greenbergian might say this is part of kitsch's trick; it doesn't blame the audience. All those Kinkade lovers are merely getting sucked into kitsch's trap; they are the *victims* of this particular story.

Yet what kind of system, the system of art, believes that those who break from the system are fools who just don't know how gullible they are? Kinkade's devotees could argue that his exclusion from the art world merely proves that its version of visual culture is fallible; they could use Judy Chicago's *The Dinner Party* as an example of a work that was deemed kitsch, then in time was elevated to art. Perhaps the difference between art and kitsch is just time.

Kinkade himself repeatedly proclaimed his outsider status, his alternative aesthetic and visual message; he did not need museums. Indeed, Kinkade may have been more popular and more sought after *because* of his stance as an outsider, certifying by extension the outsider/rebel status of his collectors. Outside, for Kinkade, was far more lucrative than inside. It was where he wanted to be.

Outside, however, can also mean visual oblivion, aggressively keeping certain objects and representations from view. From 1991 to 2009, for example, the public was essentially prohibited from viewing coffins of dead soldiers returning from the wars in Iraq and Afghanistan. Using an argument concerning privacy, President George Bush banned photographs from being taken, as had been the tradition, when bodies were taken off planes at Dover

Air Force Base. During the Vietnam War these images of flag-covered coffins had had a very negative impact on the popularity of the war, and Bush's security, communications, and legal team decided not to make the same public relations mistake twice. The images of the dead were essentially denied, made invisible.[25] If the public could not see them, if they were banished from view, they would always be outside. The ban was reversed by the Obama Administration, which opted to leave decisions about photography and the press to the families of the servicepeople. Images that had thus been pushed outside were allowed back into circulation, back into the public view.

Governments and other agents of authority work very hard to keep some images on the outside. Yet the corporate giants of social media may maintain an outside and inside far more rigidly than governments or museums ever could. Consider the provocation of #freethenipple, a hashtag for the movement that seeks to normalize images of women not wearing tops. The movement took on a particular valence in social media as Facebook, Instagram, and Twitter, for example, had very specific guidelines about the circumstances in which images of women's breasts could be posted and remain uncensored. Breastfeeding imagery, for example, is permitted in most places, but images that are merely topless or expose the areola will be removed by the sites.

In another example of the power of outside, Google has an image tab on its search bar to help the viewer find

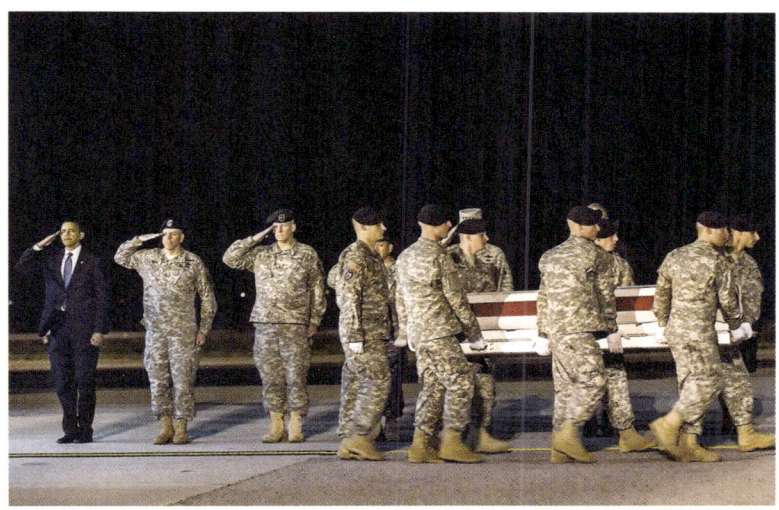

Figure 10 President Barack Obama, U.S. Army Maj. Gen. Daniel V. Wright, and Army Brig. Gen. Michael S. Repass salute as a team of soldiers carry the remains of Army Sgt. Dale R. Griffin during a dignified transfer ceremony on Dover Air Force Base, Delaware, October 29, 2009. U.S. Air Force photo by Jason Minto.

theoretically any image they could desire. Of course, these hits are all driven by algorithms that are proprietary, so the public has little sense of what images are being chosen or hidden and for what purpose. When we ask Google to search for us, we have no way to control what is "found," and no sense of *who* might have had influence over what images were chosen for viewing. To put it another way, we don't know who *wanted* us to find the images that do appear.

When we ask Google to search for us, we have no sense of *who* might have had influence over what images were chosen for viewing. To put it another way, we don't know who *wanted* us to find the images that do appear.

A common cinematic and television fantasy holds that once an image is uploaded online, it can spark a revolution of righteous justice. The world will come to its senses and see—really see—some issue that was hidden from view. Indeed, to a certain extent this has happened with videos recording police violence against black men and women, photographs of meat factories and the abuse of animals, and more local moments of justice that can be seen on the internet. Yet it must be understood that even these examples were ultimately "allowed" to be passed around by Google, Facebook, and other corporate entities. It must also be recognized that the question of permission is an international one; Google's privacy, searching, and tracking are all nation-state-specific. The internet keeps most images and audiences farther on the outside, and more estranged from each other, than might be anticipated or even readily understood. The internet is often described as a place where people can find freedom, but *where* you have access to the internet dictates what visual culture you can see and be part of.

Yet remaining outside can also be a survival technique. If visual culture can perform inclusiveness and power and belonging for those on the inside, it can also be a strategy to build a visual identity and presence that can stand in opposition. While Kinkade took on outsider status as a strategy to claim some kind of moral authority over the dialogues of visual culture and art world rules, outsider status can also bring the freedom to be isolated, ignored, left alone to create something truly unique and specific to the needs of a community. The creating of visual atmospheres outside can build community, build safety, make visible ideas that are unseen in normative visual culture. Rejected, hidden, and unseen visual atmospheres can be spaces to truly make something visually new and empowering.

The ballroom scene exemplifies this visual outsider potential. Ballroom refers to a culture that grew out of 1980s queer dance club and drag queen culture broadly, and specifically among a population of black and Latino queers living in New York City. Forming houses (essentially teams/family units), setting up competitions, dancing, walking the runway, and sharing in music and community became the hallmarks of the ballroom scene. These groups were marginalized not only from heteronormative society but from gay visual cultures that privileged white bodies and the ability to pass, or blend, when needed. According to scholar Marlon M. Bailey, ballroom culture is based on three intertwined elements, "the gender system, the kinship structure (houses), and the ball events."[26] It was the last of these, the ball events, that had the most radical impact on visual cultures and codes. The balls would feature dance and fashion runway walking as competitions within categories such as Butch Queen Realness, Femme Queen Realness, Runway, Labels, and Icons.

The ballroom scene exposes all kinds of cultural obsessions in regard to the visual. To begin with, gender is clearly and explicitly centered as a performance, an act that is constructed for an audience. The walking, the categories, the competition all remind those participating or watching that these categories are not intrinsic to a body or some origin story. Instead the ballroom demands that gender be acknowledged as a decision, an act, a space of control. Gender and sexuality are visually constructed here as categories you inhabit, know, and live, not ones that society puts on you. Realness comes from personal agency, not societal definitions.

This is, of course, an affront to normative visual culture that defines "real" gender as a set of biological markers. Just as museums create knowledge of categories that makes those categories seem inherent, so too gender is constructed around knowledges about bodies that are made to seem cohesive.

Ballroom reassigns the power to define categories and makes the visual the arbiter of realness, and the community itself the judges of that success. Authority over the body and over the visual is therefore reoriented in these spaces, and the bodies and people that are excluded, shunned, hurt, or unseen in mainstream American visual culture become the center, the core, the most visible, the most looked-at, the most praised, and the most able to articulate ideas about gender, sexuality, race, and class.

All of this was a visual play, a reordering of visual cultures that had dominated and indeed violently oppressed these communities. In the late 1980s and early 1990s, with AIDS's impact being felt and a public hysteria about the disease building, the queer body was coded in popular visual culture as the marker of a new and terrifying disease. Not surprisingly, this cultural and social backlash rained down most horrifically on black and Latinx populations. Ballroom culture became a location of visual resistance and realignment. Bodies that were marked in popular visual culture as outside would be transformed into bodies that were inside, accepted, normalized, and made to feel beautiful and seen; the outside that was the ballroom scene was the most vibrant, most liberating space for many to understand their corporeality, their identity, and their powers of resilience. The visual environment, in other words, provided freedom, space, intimacy, and community.

Outside in this context is thus a space of protection and reinvention. Invisibility in terms of cultural capital allowed a new visual dialogue to emerge, providing room for participants to see themselves in new and empowering ways. It also became a viciously smart and potent way for visual language to tear at the authorities of gender and sexuality that codified and manipulated bodies into submission. Ballroom expressed the power of performance and the radical potential of realness as an antidote to the ways in which visual culture constricts and contorts bodies.

Such an outside was perhaps too good to last. In 1990 ballroom went global in the feature documentary film

Paris Is Burning directed by Jennie Livingston, and then in Madonna's music video for *Vogue*.[27] Although filmed with different audiences and messaging in mind, both of these visual products, made and promoted by white cis-gendered women, allowed a much broader audience to look at a visual culture and language not made for them. Both the documentary and the music video were accused of cultural appropriation: both gave significant visual cultural status to their makers, and significantly less to those whose culture they featured.

This was only the beginning, and it is clear that both these works opened the door to RuPaul's *Drag Race*, a reality TV show featuring a season-long competition to be "America's next drag superstar," and Ryan Murphy's television drama *Pose* about the ballroom community in New York in the late 1980s and early 1990s. Outside, therefore, can no longer really be called outside. The communities that nurtured and created this art continue to have contested relationships to their more popular and mainstreamed offspring.

Where are we?

Inside and outside are clearly very unclear locations: the *where* of a visual object or visual meaning is slippery and moves from one meaning to the next. If thinking about the where of visual culture is so unstable, is it smarter to think where as a vortex?

Let's consider what is meant by this. A vortex is a swirl of water or air caused by changes in temperature, shifts in pressure, or discrepancies in density. In a vortex, the motion creates a momentum that both pulls objects in and disperses them according to its own physics. In terms of visual culture, and specifically of the ballroom scene, has something happened to the visual impact, the meaning, now that voguing, walking, and realness have been taken up, moved around by new bodies and identities and redistributed? And was this bound to happen? Is visual culture just a finite set of playing cards, and once we reach the end of the deck we just reshuffle and play again? Nothing is really new, nothing is really authentic or radical, everything is just fodder for the vortex and will be sucked in and eventually dropped out?

The vortex at first seems ominous, dangerous, sucking all things in and under. Perhaps we might consider the vortex a way to renegotiate the "where" of visual culture. Artist/theorist Allan deSouza asks it another way: whether we can "develop decolonizing languages *within* what would otherwise be the colonizing language of art industries."[28] The vortex, then, can be the where of the visual, never meaning one thing but always on unsteady and changing ground. Multitudes of sights may be understood as productive waves of instability, and on this flowing ground there might be space to build a new visual culture.

We might revisit the start of this chapter and the fate of Durant's sculpture as an example of the power of speaking or acting from outside. Outside was heard, and now outside is inside. Indigenous communities will be choosing other artists to speak in the public park. Outside will then be brought inside. Is this a step forward, however? Is this the long-overdue acknowledgment of talent, importance, and voice, as it was when Chicago and her *The Dinner Party* were finally taken in? Or is this more like what happened to ballroom, with a piece of a community detached and reimagined for a larger audience? In the end, the most vexing problem about visual culture is whether anything about access can be changed in this moment. As activist Gregory Sholette provocatively pushes, the "more ineffable challenge to invisibility will require more than slogans and banner drops. Yes, unquestionably, let's occupy the art world, or better yet, let's do it again comrades. And then? And then?"[29]

This provocation inevitably ends up being as much about where as about who. Indigenous protesters consistently noted that Durant's whiteness mattered. Would the piece have met with so much controversy if he had been from the community whose history he represented? This question leads us to the next chapter; where pivots to who.

3

WHO

Honey, I just wonder what it feels like in the back of your pink Cadillac.

Bruce Springsteen[1]

Provocation

By July 2008, Barack Obama's image was everywhere. He had been on countless magazines, including one for *Rolling Stone* that featured what appeared to be a halo around his head. Shepard Fairey's red, white, and blue "Hope" illustration had become ubiquitous after Super Tuesday (February). It featured a stoic Obama looking off to the side, presumably to a more promising future. In June, he had the votes to secure the Democratic Party's nomination (at the August convention) and was set to face Senator John

McCain in the general election. Obama was to be the first African American nominated by a major party to run for president and would, in November of that year, be elected the first African American president of the United States.

It was a bruising summer for Obama. He had been pushed to speak in explicit terms about his racial identity and the racial histories and tensions of the nation. This had been sparked by media attention to the speeches of Obama's former Chicago pastor, Jeremiah Wright, notably to an oft-repeated quote, said in the context of a sermon about structural racism and injustice: "God damn America." Videos uploaded to YouTube of Wright preaching and media focus on the candidate's "controversial" pastor and Wright's opinions threatened to unsettle Obama's campaign. Pressured to respond, Obama delivered what has become known as his "More Perfect Union" speech. In it, he tried to thread the very tricky needle of acknowledging the legitimate anger of many non-whites, particularly African Americans, while sticking to his consistent message of hope, reconciliation, and progress for all Americans wrapped in the dream of moving beyond the past and into a just future. By campaign measures, the speech and Obama's subsequent comments about Wright were largely successful, and by July, his campaign had steadied and the candidate was visiting several other countries to expand his foreign policy profile and feed his presidential campaign momentum.

The so-called "birther" movement coalesced and was gaining its own momentum at the same time. Germinated on the white nationalist fringes of the American right, the specious theory that Obama had not been born in the United States and was thus ineligible for the presidency in 2016 gained mainstream cultural purchase through privately funded directed campaigns and its quick embrace by several conservative television regulars. Donald Trump's path to the presidency in many ways began here when he became one of the highest-profile birther adherents.

This fringe-to-mainstream movement was rooted in vague suggestions, insinuations, and outright falsehoods alleging that Obama was not a US citizen and that he was secretly Muslim. Both charges were grounded in the underlying claim that Obama was fundamentally not American and that he (along with Muslims) represented a threat to the country. "Birther" allegations were so outrageous as to seem beyond ridiculous, yet the toxic racism, white nationalism, and Islamophobia they signaled among mainstream Americans was startling to many.

In this heated and racially charged media environment of the summer of 2008, the *New Yorker* ran a cover by cartoonist and illustrator Barry Blitt that sought to visualize the absurdity of the birther claims. Entitled "The Politics of Fear," it pictured Michelle and Barack Obama standing in the Oval Office smirking while giving each other a fist bump. Rather than his usual suit and tie, Obama wears a turban and a *shalwar kameez*, what the average American viewer might understand as clothing from the Middle East. Michelle Obama is clad in camouflage pants, combat boots, bandolier bullet belt, loosely slung machine gun, and large, Angela Davis 1969 afro; it was the look of Black Power and militancy. Next to the couple, an American flag burns in the fireplace beneath a portrait of the then-still-at-large Osama bin-Laden.

This was not the first time a *New Yorker* cover had satirized politics, nor was it Blitt's first political illustration. The magazine had a long history of using its covers, interior illustrations, cartoons, and eventually photography to transform each issue into an aesthetic object or total atmosphere marking the magazine as urbane, cosmopolitan, intellectual, and socially liberal. Tilting toward a clever, ironic style, the magazine had frequently featured cover art that was provocative, controversial, eye-catching, and political. Never as cutting as some European journals such as *Charlie Hebdo* or *Private Eye* and steering clear of the more juvenile humor of *Mad Magazine*, the *New Yorker* sought a wittier but kinder middle ground to appeal to shifting conceptions of a sophisticated US-focused intelligentsia.

The Obama cover met with quick outrage and condemnation. The official statement from the Obama campaign was: "The *New Yorker* may think, as one of their staff explained to us, that their cover is a satirical lampoon of the

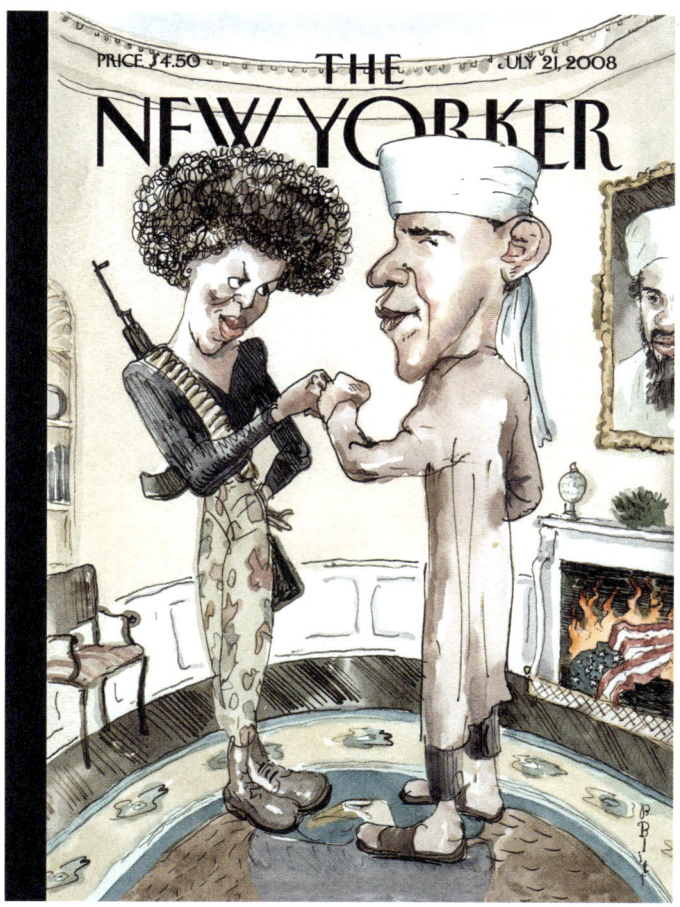

Figure 11 Barry Blitt, "The Politics of Fear," *New Yorker*, July 21, 2008. Photo credit: Barry Blitt, The New Yorker. © Conde Nast.

caricature Sen. Obama's right-wing critics have tried to create. But most readers will see it as tasteless and offensive. And we agree." The statement was promptly seconded by his opponent John McCain's campaign, which echoed that the image was "tasteless and offensive."[2] Blitt defended his cover illustration, arguing that his critics, including those with the Obama campaign, were missing the whole point: "I think the idea that the Obamas are branded as unpatriotic [let alone as terrorists] in certain sectors is preposterous. It seemed to me that depicting the concept would show it as the fear-mongering ridiculousness that it is."[3] *New Yorker* editor David Remnick supported Blitt while looking to buffer the magazine from an onslaught of negative attention and media coverage: "What I think it does is hold up a mirror to the prejudice and dark imaginings about Barack Obama's—both Obamas'—past, and their politics." He added, "it's *not* a satire about Obama—it's a satire about the distortions and misconceptions and prejudices *about* Obama."[4] Yet to many, this visualized version of the Obamas, produced and published by two white men, simply furthered the work of the white men advancing the birther movement.

Visual satire only works when the audience clearly understands that the imagery is so exaggerated and so removed from reality that it turns a corner into the absurd. It is usually difficult to describe visual satire to someone from another culture or historical period, since so much of the symbolic currency is specific to place and time. In the case of Blitt's cover, it is clear that he and Remnick presumed the imagery to be so wildly over-the-top and so obvious in its intentions that not just its direct audience but wider audiences would grasp the knowing humor and the cover's political and social commentary on race, patriotism, and Americanness.

Yet reactions clearly showed that something about the image wasn't enough. It wasn't sufficiently farcical or ironic, or far enough detached from perceptions of reality to be understood as false. This public reaction suggests that something about the image seemed to skirt precariously close—ultimately too close—to commonly held beliefs that many, including the Obama campaign, found offensive. The popular outrage over the image suggested, even before Obama's nomination and well before the birther movement would hit its true stride, that there was something very dangerous in unleashing an image that implied that the Obamas' bodies and public presentations were hiding some other dangerous reality.

In depicting a version of birthers' worst fears in order to lampoon them, had the cover illustration only made them seem more possible, more real? Had it exposed some truth in the eyes of those desperate for confirmation? Even the fist bump, a gesture the couple had done numerous times and which signaled to many both their affection for each other and their hipness, was in this image turned into a racialized symbol of an inside language or code that was fundamentally anti-white. For that is what this image speaks to, not just a fear that the Obamas are "really" something else (radicals, Muslims, anti-American), but that they deeply and violently hated white people.

The utter irony of this inversion of structural racism and centuries of physical, psychic, economic, and cultural violence perpetrated against black people by white people and white supremacist power structures did not make these fears seem obviously absurd or any less sincere. Nor did they conceal the sneaking suspicion that clung to the fear that the Obamas and all black Americans would be more than justified in such hatred. And ultimately the image was silent to the suggestion that the White House had always been a space of radical whiteness that secretly plots against non-white bodies.

Pointedly, the *New Yorker* and Blitt never apologized for the image, and Blitt continues to produce political satire for the magazine. Obama, of course, became the 44th president of the United States, and his and his family's bodies continued to represent race in ways they both embraced and actively, even aggressively, fought against. "Offensive" would remain a term that circulated around various representations of President Obama, as many organizations and individuals attempted to control the meaning of his body and his image.

Who knows

As this provocation suggests, bodies are rendered meaningful, manageable, and knowable through the visual and through acts of seeing and representing. We are fed ideas about bodies that make them visually generic, no longer specific, merely symbols. These same bodies, however, are resistant and unruly, constantly defying the authority of the gaze. At every turn we see bodies that disobey, that deny categorization and refuse the disciplining work of being stared at. But can we ever truly see each other or ourselves? Or does *the legacy of the visual* make it so that we are merely seeing shadows or stereotypes but never really a body?

While it might seem that new technologies (and I'm thinking here about virtual reality, social media, AI, and facial recognition) have only made the question of who is there more dire, I would argue this is just the newest incarnation of the fundamental paradox of visual culture: that we have never been able to truly see ourselves or anyone else. Visual culture is thus the constant, and constantly failing, attempt to replicate or transcend bodies that are trapped in racist, gender-conforming, sexist, ableist, ageist visual paradigms. The visual culture we create and recreate is often the very mechanism by which we are denied true sight, access, and empathy to other corporeal bodies. Thus, no matter what the technology and how many pictures are taken, we often have little control of how we see or are seen.

Who wants this? That's a hard question. Undoubtedly, visual culture is a record of violence, personal and political. Images of people leave lasting marks, deeply social marks, specifically on the bodies of those who are subjected to the gaze. Indeed, the very nature and meaning of the gaze is the subject of intense theorizing.[5] Is the gaze always intrusive? Can it ever be benign? Must looking always be the terrain of the explorer and the conqueror, of domination? The visual warps bodies and identities and traps people. It is this violence that we must confront if we are to forge new paths and new ways of seeing who we are. These are the questions, of who is seen and who can see, that frame this chapter.

Writer Susan Sontag famously spoke to the ethics of the visual in her popular works *On Photography* (1977) and then twenty-five years later, in the near aftermath of 9/11, in *Regarding the Pain of Others* (2003). Confronting the power of photography, or its lack, Sontag questioned whether reproducing images of war crimes, genocide, and ordinary human suffering ultimately provoked empathy or apathy. Sontag was expanding on themes with historical roots in confronting the Holocaust and the visualization of trauma, never forgetting the capacity of the visual to perpetuate trauma. Theorists Georges Didi-Huberman,

Fred Moten, Ariella Azoulay, and Jacques Rancière have all demanded a reframing of the relationship between the viewer, the subject of the image, and the image itself, all of them seeking more productive resolutions to the ways in which images damage than simply looking away. All demand that we look better, that we look with dignity and empathy, knowing that looking is a moral journey and a cultural necessity.

Of "the right to look," Mirzoeff writes,

> The right to look is not about seeing. It begins at a personal level with the look into someone else's eyes to express friendship, solidarity, or love. That look must be mutual, each person inventing the other, or it fails. . . . It means requiring the recognition of the other in order to have a place from which to claim rights and determine what is right.[6]

The right to look is also the right to be seen, but these rights, as already noted, depend on fragile agreement and equality, on the presupposition that in fact others exist and that their rights matter. We don't have that visual culture yet, and often the visual does more to trap than liberate.

But looking away has its advocates, too.[7] Turning away or refusing to look carries certain agency and can be a political act in itself, harnessed to an act of self-preservation, guilt, or both. Refusing to look might be a stance against the visual turn in academic analysis and contemporary global capitalist neoliberal culture, an argument that the visual and sight have been privileged ways of knowing that reify global inequalities to the detriment of other senses and justice.

Yet before we consider looking away, let's think a bit more on the problem of who we see.

Who am I

There is evidence that we are trying—globally and individually and very much aided by technology—to see ourselves and others in new ways. How successful these attempts are depends entirely on the definition of visual success, but personal control over one's visual domain does seem promising. If the gaze is what does the damage, it follows that millions of new people—that is, people historically denied viewership or the authority and empowerment that comes with the gaze—grabbing control of the gaze might break its power and violence.

"Selfie" is a term and a thing that did not exist twenty years ago.[8] Self-portraits existed in painting, drawing, sculpture, and photography as ways to portray subjects as they wished to look, but they tended to be labor-intensive and expensive and over time came to lack obvious appropriate places for being shown. One could, for example, set up a camera, set a timer, and take a picture with relative ease. But then the film required processing and printing, the resulting image had to be framed or mounted in some way, and then it had to be hung somewhere; and this usually meant in a private and intimate space. To surround oneself with self-portraits carried the scent of narcissism and desperation and invited ridicule or pity—just ask Dorian Gray and Norma Desmond, or one of the butts of endless film punchlines about vain actresses and over-the-top society women.

Today, the mobile phone with a camera has solved the problem of production, and various social networking platforms take care of distribution. With ease we can create visual document after visual document recording what we do, how we look, and how we want to look, and we have spaces that can accommodate these ever-growing collections of evolving visual identity markers. It is no surprise that during the same period that gave rise to the term "selfie" came the popularization of the verb "to curate" as something we all do, not just an activity for museum professionals. The *Telegraph* claimed in 2016 that worldwide, over one million selfies were taken daily, while Google revealed that same year that over 24 billion selfies had been uploaded on its platforms.[9] That's a lot of looking at faces and bodies.

Commentators on the rise of the selfie seem to fall into two general camps.[10] One perspective views the selfie in almost apocalyptic terms. We are all creatures of vanity, perhaps, but selfie critics seem to believe that the new technologies of the phone and Facebook have dramatically exacerbated this quality. For them, the selfie is linked to narcissism and nihilism, self-interest and a lack of empathy, which also results in lack of self-confidence. Worse yet, critics frame selfies as a "contagion" that can move from person to person, screen to screen.[11] Popular magazine articles consider the various psychological issues you could be avoiding or indulging with your selfie habit. There are ways to diagnose yourself to see if you are suffering from "selfitis."[12] This take on the selfie is also generationally focused, their elders seeing young people as living to primp, click, and post instead of living life. Ubiquitous and pathologized, the selfie is thus evidence of more profound social dysfunctions: the visual is literally making you sick, distorting your view, making you incapable of seeing yourself or anyone else.

Advocates for the selfie see the stakes as being just as high, if to different ends. In her *Hashtag Authentic*, Sara Tasker sees the selfie and its attendant digital platforms as nothing short of a vision revolution. "In human history, there have been too few voices with little diversity. Women, people of color, people with disabilities, and a great many others have found themselves rendered invisible"; the selfie allows for representational democracy that humans have never had access to before, or as Tasker puts it, "we're not playing by the old rule book and we're not telling the stories that we have always been told."[13] The selfie, for Tasker and others, is proof of the potential of a new world order, one that is built on *visibility*. Technology, in this case, has made right an injustice and allowed individuals to assert their authentic selves. More selfies, many argue, means more diversity, more democracy, and more people seeing and being seen.

What both sides of this debate take for granted is that selfie takers want to be, and believe that they are, in control of their image; that through repetition of images, getting the right angle, and using the right props or poses, something stable, controllable, and true is created. From either point of view, the selfie reveals an increasingly global belief in the power of visual culture and the power of the individual to control their place in it. I was here. I do exist. Who am I? Well, here I am!

Kim Kardashian West is a central figure of this visual selfie movement. Loathe her or love her, the reality show celebrity demonstrates the power of the selfie, standing as a sort of ambassador from the world of self-fashioning and self-branding, emblematic of the power, wealth, and the ability to be seen that selfie culture promises. (To others she is a cautionary tale, or a sign that it is already too late.) Her selfies are fundamental connections with her fans and the world, perhaps the most crucial aspect of her self/brand marketing. Her selfies tell us who she wants us to see. So important is this identification and so vast her archive that in 2015 Kardashian West published a collection of the images, in coffee table art book style, called *Selfish*. It was a *New York Times* bestseller. The very idea that these images could and should be transported from their online location and digital medium to the form of an art book signifies the meaning Kardashian West and others have placed on the value, monetarily and culturally, of looking at her self-created images of herself. In a popular culture saturated with Kardashians and their satellites, is the value of Kim's selfies grounded in their promise of behind-the-scenes authenticity, made and controlled by her? Or is the whole *Selfish* project one enormous inside joke, a monetized moment of poking fun at oneself and the culture?

To grasp the full meaning of *Selfish* and its creator, we need to step back and consider Kim Kardashian West's longer history and celebrity journey. The universally agreed-upon point of origin for her megacelebrity is the internet release of a sex tape in 2007 by porn industry giant Vivid Entertainment. The tape had been privately recorded when Kim was twenty-two years old. When she learned of the tape's sale, Kardashian West sued to stop its release and insisted she had no knowledge of, or role in, its sale. The lawsuit was settled within weeks, and in April 2007 Vivid Entertainment released the 41-minute film with the title *Kim Kardashian, Superstar*. Her family's reality show, *Keeping Up with the Kardashians*, debuted six months later on the E! channel.

Kardashian West's rise to notoriety and then fame came from this moment of exposure. The pornographic blurring of public and private life was framed explicitly, and the video was sold as having been done without her consent. This moment may have signaled the danger of the addictive promise of fame, riches, power, and "free" agency to be found in a world of surveillance capitalism and degraded forms of consent.

Kardashian West did not hide in shame or retreat from her quest for celebrity in 2007, but turned one moment of exposure into a perpetually exposed life and career, for herself and many others. She was relentless in her self-promotion, pushing her body and developing brand into as many visual platforms as possible, from traditional celebrity print media to television and even films. The foundation of her saturating fame, however, was always the internet and social media and the performance of a direct, "real" connection to her fans/consumers. Kardashian West was an early adopter of Instagram, constantly feeding it content, mostly images of her face and her scantily clad body. The sex tape is still available for viewing, but has become in many ways the least exposing or intimate footage of Kardashian West available. She seized the very mechanisms that had robbed her of control to swamp them with her own story. The selfie represents her reclamation of the gaze, her empowerment as an agent of her own narrative, rather than the object in someone else's. For at its base, the tale of Kardashian West is about gender and women.

In his groundbreaking 1972 visual culture manifesto *Ways of Seeing*, John Berger wrote, "A woman must continually watch herself. She is almost continually accompanied by her own image of herself. . . . Men act and women appear."[14] Feminist scholars have pushed and pulled at this idea, yet the female body—watched, drawn, photographed, painted, filmed, and streamed—has been the core object of Western art and visual practices for centuries. The female form is freighted, always, by exposure, by expectation, judgment, and the act of being looked at.

I hesitate to call Kardashian West a feminist rebel, freedom fighter, or iconoclast in her reimagining and self-depiction of her own form and her relation to larger trends in the consumption of the female body. She came to public consciousness through sexual exploitation (one that by her telling was a violation), but her self-produced images only double down and expand on the video version of "Kim Kardashian West." She presents her body as a site of consumption and pleasure for others. She twists, bends over, and poses. Her images all train the gaze to her hips, ass, and breasts; if to her face, her mouth is often slightly open, suggestively inviting, just like her gaze as she looks at you looking at her.

The female form is freighted, always, by exposure, by expectation, judgment, and the act of being looked at.

In taking hold of the visual dialogue of the selfie, she has taken her body, which was made available for the sexual consumption of everyone by Vivid Entertainment, and then repeatedly sexualized her own body *with her own hands*. In this way she has weaponized and monetized for herself the ways women and their bodies have historically been contained and manipulated to evoke pleasure for men, a pleasure that was often taken from women without their consent and certainly rarely to their benefit, especially monetarily. Additionally, she has reimagined and adjusted this vision into new phases of her life, as mother and business executive.

Critically, Kardashian West's work is done through a medium that requires the viewer to acknowledge her own hand in the making. She seldom edits out of the pictures her stretched hand holding the phone, or hides that she is looking in a mirror to take the picture. If anything, these details are crucial to her image-making. The viewer is meant to understand this, because then they can see her in the actual physical act of making the image. Who is in control? Well, whoever is taking the picture. Thus, she visually reminds the viewer that she is managing their access. As journalist Ruth Curry notes, "Kim Kardashian makes money on the labor women have been historically asked to do for free."[15] Indeed, the Kardashians are all very attentive to the heretofore "hidden" aspects of feminine grooming and display. Having everyone look at you takes work, and the selfie, in fact, documents this labor. Kardashian West destroys the fantasy of the woman's body as natural. The selfie is, at base, an image of labor. She is working, and you are watching her work. (It is also not outrageous to suggest that through this kind of marketing and success Kardashian West has birthed the now ubiquitous form of the YouTube makeup tutorial, hair styling videos, and other self-care entertainment, whose significance and popularity lie in lifting the veil from what was previously known only to the very rich and famous. It is also worth noting that most of these newly monetized YouTube stars are women, queers, and people of color, suggesting that Kardashian West's influence has opened the doors to others who have historically been outside of the sphere of producing, and being paid for, visual content.)

A sticking point for many in this reading of Kardashian West is that she and her mother may have been the original architects of the sex tape's sale and that her claims to violation were only part of the performance. This charge has been made so often and in so many ways that it has taken on the sheen of truth, despite continued denials from the Kardashians. But the conflict between "guilt" and "innocence," "strategic" or "victimized," remains visually narrated through Kardashian West's body. It replicates much older misogynist claims that women aren't violated because they always want to be seen, desired, exposed; their consent is always implied, even when they say "No."

The power of the gaze is always authorized by patriarchy, even when turned against it.

Consider another American example of this kind of resistance. In 2014, Columbia University student Emma Sulkowicz began to carry a twin-bed mattress around campus and to classes in a performance piece later called *Carry That Weight*. Sulkowicz (who uses them/they/their pronouns) was raped in their second year of college and began dragging the heavy and unwieldy mattress during senior year as a public marker of the incident, as an act to confront Columbia University's refusal to expel the rapist, and as their senior thesis and art performance. It is likely that the performance's reach would have been largely local had it not been for the countless videos and still images of Sulkowicz carrying the mattress uploaded to YouTube, Twitter, Facebook, and Instagram. The viral circulation of the performance and Sulkowicz's story brought them to the attention of the likes of famed fellow performance artist Marina Abramović and feminists such as art critic Roberta Smith of the *New York Times* and Senator Kirsten Gillibrand, who was fighting at the time for more recognition of the problem of sexual assault and violence against women in the military.

This is to say, Sulkowicz's image, their body, and particularly their body struggling under the weight of the mattress were visualized in ways that transcended either a typical performance art piece or an act of student protest.

The images and Sulkowicz themselves came to stand in for the brave self-empowerment of sexual assault survivors, of refusing to be silent and taking back the narrative and control of one's body. Speaking to the Women's Leadership Forum of the Democratic National Committee in 2014 and soon to announce her decision to run for the presidency again, former Secretary of State Hillary Clinton said that the picture of Sulkowicz carrying the mattress should "haunt all of us."[16]

Seeing the performance in person or online made the weight of sexual violence itself seeable. This is particularly notable given the relative paucity of mainstream images depicting rape, a point made by visual theorist Ariella Azoulay with her provocative query, "has anyone ever seen a photograph of a rape?" Images exist, of course, but, as Azoulay notes, the isolation of sexual assault from other forms of violence is reinforced by the general taboo against exhibiting such images. The taboo stems from a complex and contradictory set of moral positions that seek to not further an assault by representationally repeating it, but often privilege most the (presumed) sensitivities of the viewer. This results in the broad "effacement of rape," giving rape the power of being unvisualizable. Deeming it too awful to see, according to Azoulay, only furthers a narrow gendered dialogue about this violence that effectively erases it.[17]

Sulkowski's performance charges headlong into this visual lacuna, as did the selfie-inspired "Project

Unbreakable," a Tumblr site (2011–2015) collecting the selfies of sexual assault survivors overlaid with text of the things said to them by their abusers.[18] Azoulay's analysis would seem crucial here. Are both performances, while empowering, ultimately replications of the visual silences surrounding rape? Does this aftereffect, traumatic residue, and the demonstrable possibilities for resilience distort the visual culture of rape and the potential for a feminist reevaluation of control of the body?

To pull Sulkowicz into conversation with Kardashian West is not to minimize the former or elevate the latter; it is to draw out the shared gendered, contextual, technological, and distributional conditions of their creations and assertions of agency and control. Both makers manipulate the very visual vocabularies of accessibility and normative conceptions of gender, sexuality, and power that have facilitated the objectification and exploitation of women and the female form for centuries. Both want their version of who they are to have power through circulation.

That Kardashian West and Sulkowicz do so, in part, by stepping into the gendered roles of "victim" and certain displays of normative weakness highlights their other central common trait: privilege. Both figures' racial, economic, and social status, and the avenues of access these furnished, provided the necessary foundations upon which their rebellions were conceivable and were built. This is exactly the kind of access and horizon of possibility that have been so often denied to most women and to the gender-nonconforming who are non-white, poor, have disabilities, or are not Americans, among other things. Their status also allowed them to be seen as feminized innocents who had been wronged. In the end, *Carry That Weight* only makes sense if Sulkowicz visibly struggles with the mattress and its movement. The visual message necessarily highlights the fragility, weakness, and vulnerability of bodies that are presumed to be female.

New technologies of visual culture seem to promise new freedoms and potential forms of justice in providing platforms for more voices, more agency, and more ability to forge new narratives. But if Kardashian West and Sulkowicz find heroic ways to slip some of the traps of their embodied representations, their very success highlights just how difficult it is to reclaim the body from *all* the traps. This is to say, while Kardashian West and Sulkowicz manipulate visual culture to reclaim individual authority and control and claim the technology of surveillance as a means of empowerment, both ultimately resort to rearticulating and thus reifying extant gender categories. We can perhaps see who they are, but this depends on visual strategies that obscure who others might be. The promise that this new individual power of the visual will aid in breaking the larger patterns, that we all will *see* ourselves and each other in new and truer ways, simply doesn't hold.

Who can see

Recently a landmark case about visual culture and property—about ownership and who gets to look—was heard in a Massachusetts courtroom. On March 20, 2019, Tamara Lanier sued Harvard University for payment of "unspecified punitive and emotional damages" for the theft of an image and cruel "dominion" over its uses. Lanier filed the suit on behalf of her enslaved relatives Renty and Delia, a father and daughter of whom a series of daguerreotypes were taken in 1850 in South Carolina. The daguerreotypes formed part of the research of Louis Agassiz, a storied nineteenth-century naturalist who founded Harvard's Museum of Comparative Zoology and was a fierce advocate of the scientific hypothesis that people of color were biologically inferior to whites. Agassiz's collection of images remained in the university's archives unseen until they were rediscovered in the mid-1970s. As some of the earliest known photographs of enslaved people in the United States, the images were of immediate interest to scholars and other authors; Harvard monitored their distribution with sharp attention to copyright law. Records show careful attention to permissions and payment collections for reproducing the images, including threatening to sue those who did not follow proper channels.

In other words, Harvard used the images as it saw fit and made a profit from their circulation (which is standard legal practice). This formed the basis of Lanier's claim. Harvard could not really own these images, her case held, because as enslaved people, Renty and Delia could not have given their consent to be photographed. The original images had been stolen first by Agassiz and then the crime was sustained and magnified by Harvard University.

Property and ownership were central to the case but did not form the heart of Lanier's charges, which centered on the violence of visual culture and the trauma dispersed across generations because of it. As a descendant of the enslaved people depicted in the photos, Lanier described her own violation by the images. As writer and scholar Ta-Nehisi Coates noted, "That photograph is like a hostage. . . . This is an enslaved black man with no choice being forced to participate in white supremacist propaganda—that's what that photograph was taken for."[19] Thus, what Harvard wielded was not just power over an object and the rights to its reproduction, but the power to inflict recurring harm on a family.

Indeed, the daguerreotypes are by any measure haunting and intense. Renty and Delia are posed in each image stripped to their waists, facing forward, and looking directly into the camera. They were being photographed by Agassiz as exemplar types, to be studied not as individuals but as generic specimens. While it is doubtful they were aware of the reach of the dehumanizing and genocidal visual language they were being translated into, their body language and facial expressions suggest that their images were taken under duress.

This contemporary legal case centers a growing cultural dialogue about what images do to people in the context of structural inequality and the continued violations, humiliations, and murderous violence exacted on black bodies. The case drew energy and argumentative power from the visual exploitation that followed the police murder of Michael Brown in Ferguson, Missouri, that launched the Black Lives Matter movement. After he was killed, the eighteen-year-old Brown's body was left in the middle of a residential street, uncovered for over an hour until he was draped with a sheet by a paramedic. The corpse remained unshielded for about three more hours. In addition to forcing residents of the street to confront the body, the interval allowed individuals and news teams to photograph and film at will. There seemed no end to appetites for the visual consuming, examining, and distributing of black bodies.

Lanier's case demands that Harvard stop circulating her ancestors' images to the university's financial gain and resolve that this cannot be another instance of black people being bought and sold, viewed, and discarded. In challenging the university's rights to the image, she makes alternative claims to ownership and self-possession. Who sees, Lanier's case suggests, needs to be bound to whose history, bodies, and pain are on view.

The case also carries echoes of the controversy that erupted at the 2017 Whitney Biennial, which included a painting called *Open Casket* by the white American artist Dana Schultz. It was based on the famous 1955 photograph of Emmitt Till's mutilated young face taken at his Chicago funeral.[20] The picture itself represents a key moment of black activism through visual culture, as well as an instance of familial ownership and parental authority. Till's mother, Mamie Till-Mobley, famously resisted the overwhelming sentiment that she should give her tortured and lynched son a closed-casket funeral so that no one could see his injuries. She refused, she said, because people *had to see* what those white men in Mississippi had done to her child. Horrifying photographs showing Till's brutalized face were published nationally by *Jet* magazine and others, catalyzing a generation of activists for civil rights and racial justice. But notions of collectively owned trauma became fraught when claimed, or co-opted, by a white artist. Activists and many contemporary artists and critics took offense at what they saw as Schultz's claiming of that image and history for her own gains, her own pleasures and pains, her own artistic expression and fame—or visibility. The question of the visual ownership and stewardship of black pain repeats.

The question is crucial because it requires us to ask what should be done with these visual documents of pain and trauma, and who gets to decide. Saidiya Hartman argues in *Scenes of Subjection* (1997) that the circulation of depictions of slavery (literary and visual) reproduces its dehumanizations, meaning that the dead are never safe from the living. The enslaved body is perpetually violated, manipulated as evidence for racist ideologies of white supremacy. The medium and the nature of the visual extend this manipulation indefinitely. Unless someone stops it, and unless we as viewers stop culturally desiring to see the black body in submission and pain.

Maybe this is really a photography problem, as photography found ways to further perpetuate and concretize racism. Photography in its early days promised to be a new, more truthful version of seeing. Hence the old saw, "the camera never lies." Only that was never really the case; camera tricks were an almost immediate result of the new technology. But as scholar Tom Gunning smartly notes, "No one fakes a photograph unless they want someone to believe it; a forgery or counterfeit depends on the assumption of authority."[21] The photograph had this authority; this was exactly the reason Agassiz and so many others sought to construct stable and objective systems of knowledge about the modern world through photography. It was, in fact, a deeply valuable tool in which "proof" of racial theories and racial injustice, not to mention other ideas about gender, sexuality, ability, and all corporeal differences, could be recorded, studied, stared at, and interpreted. Photography thus becomes a tool to see difference, to code bodies, to categorize, naturalize, and normalize the ideas of race and racial injustice.

Even more insidiously, cameras were quite literally manufactured not to "see" color of skins, not to define the breadth of human tonality. Whiteness was the baseline, and all other shades were framed around this center, making a diversity of colors almost impossible to achieve. As scholar Sarah Lewis argues, "By categorizing light skin as the norm and other skin tones as needing special corrective care, photography has altered how we interact with each other without us realizing it."[22] The very same problem of visibility—literally the ability of people of color to be seen in color photographs—was then replicated in film. It is commonplace now for actors of color to discuss how hard it is for them to find makeup and hair artists who know how to enhance non-white skin for film. Similarly, lighting was a constant issue for non-white actors; only the increase in movies and television shows featuring non-white actors has created a visual demand for proper lighting. What we have been viewing was created with technology made to disappear and distort all non-white bodies.

If the move to computers seemed to promise a liberation from the corporeal and all the old discriminations that preceded it, such fantasies were quickly squelched. A staggering amount of data points to deeply discriminatory practices at the roots of computer science and data algorithms. At each step of coding—done by humans with explicit and implicit biases—systems of data collection and processing replicate older systems of categorization, division, and invisibility that produced our racial, gendered, and class systems of knowledge and communication. As digital scholar Clemens Apprich reminds us, "This is why in computer science 'pattern discrimination' is still used as a technical term to describe the imposition of identity on input data, in order to alter (i.e., to discriminate) information from it. But far from being a neutral process, the delineation and application of patterns is in itself a highly political issue, even if hidden behind a technical terminology."[23] Even the burgeoning field of artificial intelligence has been revealed to ignore or be unable to recognize non-white faces. Activist and computer programmer Joy Buolamwini has termed this the "coded gaze" and mobilized an online community, the Algorithmic Justice League, to try to combat this new permutation of the old problems of visibility, race, and gender.

In this sense, both Buolamwini and Lanier are after the same thing: to take back power, to take back control from visual images that threaten to run further away, twisting and distorting as they go. But are they both fighting an unwinnable battle? Will non-white bodies always be trapped, undressed, unseen, and dehumanized? Will whiteness visually always signify a power to be seen and paradoxically to be unmarkable and unbound? Does visual culture, in short, prevent seeing past race?[24]

If the move to computers seemed to promise a liberation from the corporeal and all the old discriminations that preceded it, such fantasies were quickly squelched. A staggering amount of data points to deeply discriminatory practices at the roots of computer science and data algorithms.

Whose past, whose future?

Culture and ideas about the self are not made somewhere else and then simply processed by the visual tools of propaganda. We experiment and try to see so that we can reflect, so we can understand. Visual culture leads the way to knowledge; to give up on this aspect of our humanity is not ever as easy as simply hiding, banning, censoring, or smashing. As Allahyari's *King Uthal* reminds us, even if we smash something, it comes back around.

Then how do we make better bodies? Is there a way to see bodies as less triggering and destructive? Can we make a visual atmosphere we can share and thrive in where we can experiment with who we are?

Some of the most interesting theories on sight confront these questions, and do so with a recognition that the past must be part of the future. To deny the legacy of all those paintings, photographs, poorly lit films, and even the newly diabolical AI would fundamentally ignore the tenaciousness of visual culture. It stays in systems, no matter how hard we might try to flush it out. Some visual makers look to repurpose old, broken, and evil tools in order to reveal their machinations and terrible effects, and to offer new possibilities. As curator Johanna Burton hopefully suggests, "it is toward this idea of the impossible as a space of potential, and a place of *other* futures," that we should seek to move.[25] This isn't desperation, or senseless abandon, but thoughtful confrontation with the past and future of the body and its representations.

This desire for "other futures" is again what Mirzoeff wants from the "right to look." But he cautions that this right "must be mutual, each person inventing the other, or it fails." For Mirzoeff, all kinds of people, corporations, governments, social injustices are trying to control your look, directing your gaze, or telling you to "look away." He wants another path in which those controlling mechanisms are broken and instead we engage in a mutual looking and a mutual willingness to be seen.[26]

Mickalene Thomas might offer such a path forward. Thomas is most recognized as a painter, yet her work extends to photography, installation, and film. Regardless of material, her art returns relentlessly to the black female body, visual territory that, as we have discussed, has been twisted, turned, used, and reframed by artists and other makers for centuries.[27] Particularly in modern and contemporary European and American art (and thus also in the global view), the black female body has been perhaps the most manipulated, hyperexposed, and erased human form. Black women are made to represent just about everything except themselves; they are made oversexed, maternally asexual, matriarchal, made empty, vicious, or angry, made servile—black women have been made into everything and nothing within visual culture. For Thomas to confront this representational body—which is also her body—is not only to take on the very inability of imagery to speak to "real" experience and diverse humanity, as Mirzoeff promises, but also to wade through all the various ghosts of the past that threaten to devour any new representational forms.

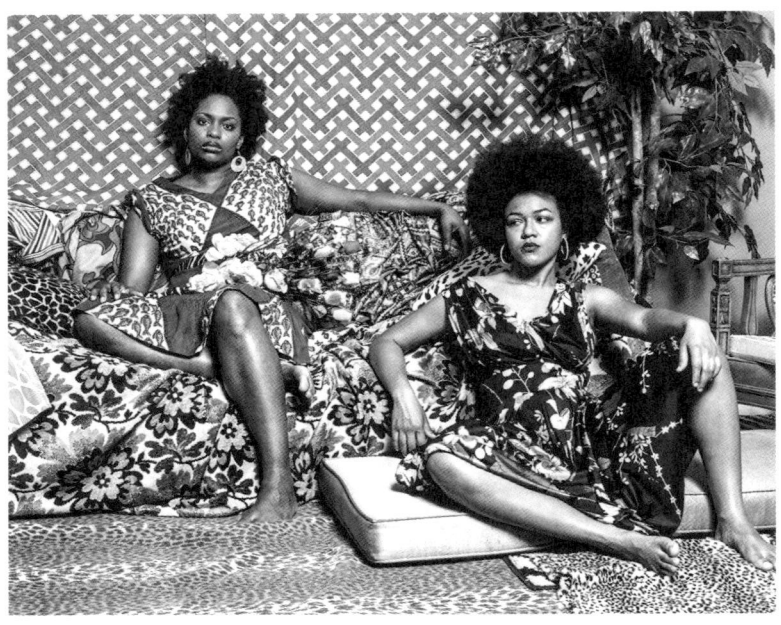

Figure 12 Mickalene Thomas, *A Moment's Pleasure in Black and White*, 2008. Fiber print, overall 23¾ × 29¾ × ³⁄₁₆ in. (60.3 × 75.6 × 0.5 cm). Purchase with funds from the Photography Committee. Whitney Museum of American Art, New York. © 2019 Mickalene Thomas / Artists Rights Society (ARS), New York. Digital image © Whitney Museum of American Art / Licensed by Scala / Art Resource, NY.

Thomas's strategy is to find and depict the "real" through the history of the not real. Her black-and-white photographic work *A Moment's Pleasure in Black and White* (2008) shows two black women. One sits on a couch with her knee kicked up, leaning back comfortably as she stares directly at the viewer, unsmiling. The second woman is at her feet, seated on a cushion on the floor, her legs spread with her dress draped to cover the space between; her arms are relaxed and mimic the position of the arms of the woman on the couch. The second woman turns her head almost in profile as she looks off past the camera. The room they are in is crowded with plants, pillows, rugs, blankets, and curtains, all with materials in contrasting patterns. The rug has a leopard print, the couch and one woman's dress are flowered, the curtain and pillow have geometric designs. The space is so crowded with pattern and imagery that at first glance one might miss the bouquet of flowers in the lap of the woman on the couch, not held, rather just placed there for effect.

It is the flowers that set Thomas's visual argument in motion. The flowers draped just so, a bouquet offered to the casually presented female figure, would to many evoke Édouard Manet's *Olympia* (1863, Musée d'Orsay). That painting, which many credit with beginning the modern turn in European art, shows a prostitute reclining nude on a couch and being presented with a bouquet of flowers by her black maid. Simultaneously, Thomas's image with the two women sitting legs spread alludes to Henri Matisse's numerous paintings featuring black and Middle Eastern women luxuriating in harem-like settings. Matisse—a contemporary of Picasso in pushing for a new kind of painting—sought a detachment, a new beauty, an emptiness in the bodies of non-white women. Their forms allowed him to play with pattern and to disassemble form and pattern and paint on the canvas. Both Matisse and Manet were pulling from even older traditions of showing women as available, decorative, and inconsequential.

It is too easy to say that Thomas reclaims these bodies from art history and from white artists like Matisse and Manet. Her line of vision here also runs to images from the Black Panthers, the Harlem Renaissance, Angela Davis's afro (as we saw on Michelle Obama in the Blitt illustration), and blaxploitation films of the 1970s. Even in those moments that asserted black self-determination, liberation, and beauty, black women were often framed as mostly decorative, mostly available, mostly for easy visual consumption. In short, Thomas makes overt and subtle challenges in the photograph to the very long, very fraught history of looking at black female bodies.

To say this is merely a rearticulation of these tropes, however, is to miss the whole point. Thomas is going after much harder visual work. She produces this image not simply to destabilize dominant conceptions of the black female body or to show black women possessing the power of the gaze. She does this work *through* the entwined white and black histories of misrepresentation, objectification, coerced performances of submission, and gendered expectations. Thomas wants the viewer to see and know several contradictory things at once, which one might argue approximates the experience of being a Black woman in America. She reminds us that these bodies in similar poses and settings—in other paintings, photographs, sculptures, and films—have been rendered inconsequential and nearly invisible in their hypervisibility and caricature. At the same time, Thomas wants us to see their beauty, strength, and human appetites. The *who* of these women matters. To twist the point even further, she wants the viewer to consider their own visual appetites for these women in this scene and their meanings, while making clear her own desires as a queer black woman. The title, *A Moment's Pleasure*, pushes the viewer to think about the moment of the picture, the present moment of looking at it, and the pleasure in both. Desire and strong appetites—historical, contemporary, and in the future—move through the visual atmosphere of this work, refusing to settle. Scholars Huey Copeland and Krista Thompson have described this atmosphere as the "Afrotrope," which names the repeating patterns, memories, and visual forms of black arts that "materialize and are about time—its passage and return . . . in response to differing social, political, and institutional conditions that inform the experiences of black people as well as changing historical perspectives of blackness."[28]

The purposeful disjunctures and contrivances produced in this work disrupt its chronological and visual cohesiveness. The viewer is thus unable to move easily through the image but is actively disoriented, tossed around. Hito Steyerl frames this type of disconnect as a way to create chaos that does not allow the viewer to rely on traditional, pleasurable, and already "known" visual information about bodies and meaning. She writes, "we can reedit the parts that were cut—whole countries, populations, even whole parts of the world, of films and videos that have been cut and censored because they do not conform to ideas of economic viability and efficiency. We can edit them into incoherent, artificial, and alternative political bodies."[29] For Steyerl, the incoherent is exactly what creates new visual potential. Thomas reassembles imagery to create a liberating chaos. The black woman thus becomes a new, unknowable body, connected to and yet untethered from history. In that new location might be a visual freedom.

A similar visual strategy is at work in the popular visual and political spectacle *Hamilton: The Musical* by Lin-Manuel Miranda. Premiering on Broadway in 2015, the musical is ostensibly about Alexander Hamilton's unlikely journey to becoming a "Founding Father" of the United States. It is, in fact, a rumination on race, immigration, history, and memory. The other conceit of the musical is that all of the "real" historical figures who were white, save for the king of England, are portrayed by black, Latinx, and Asian actors. Additionally, while the actors wear costumes appropriate to the eighteenth century, their music and choreography blends traditional musical theater forms with rap, hip hop, and R&B.

The radical disruption created by the visual spectacle—and it is important to keep in mind that the impact can only

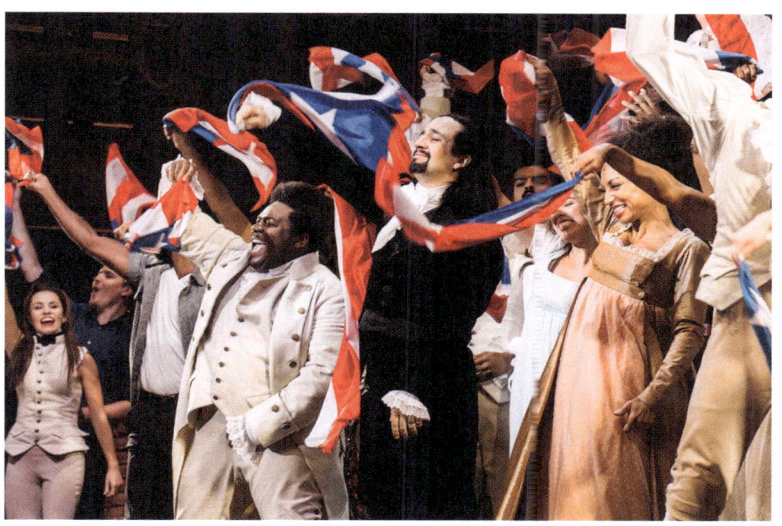

Figure 13 Emilio Madrid, *Photograph of Hamilton Cast in Puerto Rico*, 2019. Digital photograph. Image courtesy of the artist.

be understood visually—rests in swapping in non-white bodies for historically white ones, and thus diversifying the historical narrative. It is, in that sense, a visual overwriting of history. The musical's casting seizes the representational authority of the Founding Fathers' whiteness (if not their maleness) to infuse foundational myths and notions of the American promise with celebrations of new immigrant hustle and love of adopted nation.

Given the tremendous success of *Hamilton*, this overwriting cannot be dismissed as just a one-off pop culture moment. Miranda's musical has won countless awards in the United States and abroad and sold millions of theater tickets and original-cast recordings; its creator and other cast members were featured for over a year on late-night TV, awards shows, daytime programming, and print magazines and sparked dynamic national political and academic debate. Since then, the play has toured continuously in the United States and abroad.

This strategy of visual replacement, supplanting, and reediting did not meet with universal appeal. Historian Lyra D. Monteiro, for example, pointed out that in this musical that looked to reimagine the great white men of history, there was barely any mention of slavery, and no enslaved or free black speaking character.[30] Also problematic is that the actual role of non-white people in the revolutionary founding of America gets no mention. Thus, for Monteiro, in making the central visual strategy one of featuring non-white bodies as protagonists at the center of a singular narrative of history there is a missed opportunity both to disrupt this narrative and to recognize non-white people's part in the history all along.

Rearranging, cutting, disorientation, however, all remain interesting strategies both to get the viewer out of a traditional gaze and to inhibit the body being looked at from fitting into any narrow, preconceived notion. The problem is that this way requires bringing back and knowing all that visual history, all those past bad stories, to get the impact of the new bodies. Yet Thomas and Miranda clearly see no other way but through the body, for all its trouble.

Who is left?

Others have attempted to forgo the body in the hope of shifting viewers' relationships with theirs and others' bodies. Considering the body means considering boundaries, which means considering contested citizenship and national belonging. How bodies shift in meaning, moving from legal to illegal when they cross an imaginary line, is a most vexing pressure on visualizing the self and its surroundings. Even the language used—immigrant, migrant, refugee, displaced, undocumented, exile, noncitizen—suggests a fundamental inability to represent clearly the processes of bodies moving, under duress or otherwise.

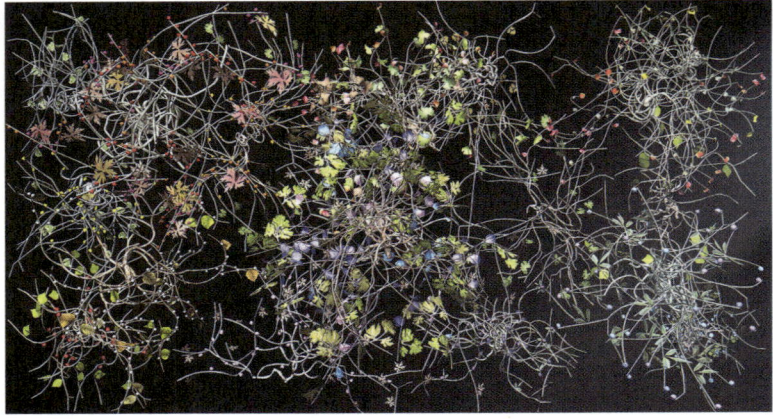

Figure 14 Jennifer Steinkamp, *Diaspore 1*, 2014, installation view at "Jennifer Steinkamp: Blind Eye," Clark Art Institute, Williamstown, Massachusetts, 2018. Courtesy the artist and Lehmann Maupin, New York, Hong Kong, and Seoul. Photo: Jennifer Steinkamp.

The video work of Jennifer Steinkamp, notably her *Diaspore 1* (2014), seeks just this sort of unpacking. The viewer first confronts a chaotic-looking plane of loosed flower petals, leaves, branches, and roots moving around the large screen on which they are projected, as if blown by a slow wind. Patterns emerge, clumps form, but nothing coheres recognizably before the individual petals and sticks start to break off and move to an opposite side of the screen or retreat back to earlier clumps. The movements seem random, and yet there is a rhythmic flow to the work that quickly become mesmerizing and naturalized. The title, a twist on the way plants disperse their spores, is also a reference to how people move, in diasporas, from one edge of the world to the other and back again. People migrate, congregate, but also get thrown out of their path by random boundaries. This movement is both generative and yet in Steinkamp's visual version also disorienting, and control is denied at all points.

Likewise, the materiality of the piece as a computer-generated video projection demands that the viewer consider nature, the machine, and the body as all being linked and pushed and pulled in ways that generate their own patterns and internal dynamics. Yet the objects that get spun around the screen also run into the boundaries of the screen itself, bouncing off their trajectory and then being smashed into other groups that had formed. The walls prohibit truly free movement and force pieces out of their path and into the path of other objects. Again, there are no bodies, no people, no faces, no discrete reference to either contemporary or long-standing effects of boundaries, refugees, or the rise in anti-immigrant sentiment globally, but that is still the visual point.[31] If viewers cannot see the myriad images of bodies and people washed up on shores or trapped in refugee camps, if these ways of photographing and telling the story of displacement and migration have no effect, Steinkamp is suggesting another kind of vision, another kind of weaponry to get at the body.

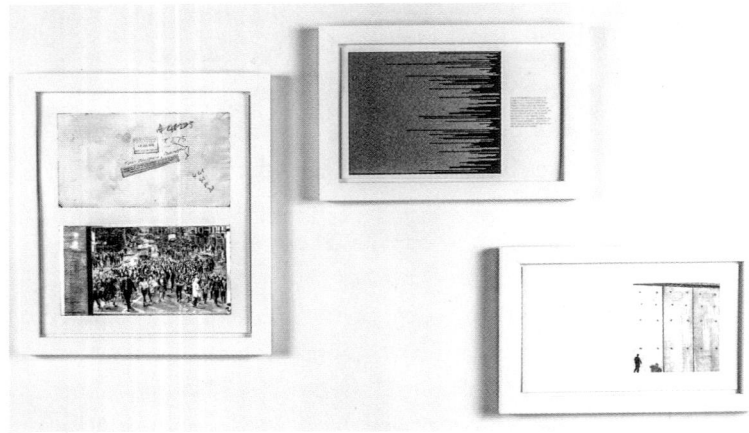

Figure 15 Brian Bishop, *Untitled (Rumination on Borders I)*, 2019. Archival pigment print, graphite, color pencil, and gouache on paper, 48 × 26 in. (122 × 66 cm). Image courtesy of the artist.

Artist Brian Bishop attacks the same visual crisis with a different strategy. His work *Untitled (Rumination on Borders I)* (2019) features four sections, the first two being drawings of the front and back of a photograph taken for the *Daily Photograph* of a march down the Falls Road, Belfast marking the end of the Falls Curfew in 1970. The Curfew exacerbated the violence between the occupying British Army and the Irish Republican Army (IRA), in a pivotal moment of the Troubles. The third image is comprised of the source code for a photograph of United States President Donald Trump, when he was arguing the value of borders and walls in a celebration of Brexit, which threatens to reestablish the hard boundary between Northern Ireland and Ireland that was the crux of decades of violence and thousands of deaths. The final image is a drawing of one of the prototypes that was made of the wall that President Trump wants to extend across the border between Mexico and the United States.

Bishop speaks, on one level, to memory, journalism, and the legacy of the photo. Photography—the source of so much consternation and the technology that crystalized fears of imagery fundamentally disabling empathy—in Bishop's hands seems simultaneously disposable and not powerful enough yet too close, too visually oppressive, too damning. The photograph, of women and children delivering bread to the victims of the Curfew, is reanimated in Bishop's work by being drawn. This act of transcribing the original photograph thus pulls the image out of history so that the grief and activism of the bodies can be seen anew. Drawing both the front and the back of the photograph reminds the viewer of the tactility of memory, the thingness of photography. Scholar Kobena Mercer suggests that photographs have a "diasporic life of their own."[32] Mercer also posits that when these images begin their new life as art is also the point when "their latent futurity is actualized." They become, in other words, more themselves, more part of a future as opposed to being stuck in a never-quite-there, incomplete past. Bishop enhances that view, making the photograph more, marking how it can move between boundaries, streets, and time periods. Yet the two adjoining images, both relating to the divisive Trump, Bishop literally walls off: the first by transmuting an image to digital code, the second by overdrawing the digital prototype of the wall, making it abstract and thus not as specifically vicious. Bishop suggests here that Trump is too much to take in, too graphic an image, too obscene, and that the viewer should be shielded from him and his legacy. This is he whose image—whose vision—we must not speak or see.

Like Steinkamp and indeed Thomas and Miranda, Bishop attempts to communicate around the body and through the body, to both engage with and then also cast off the past embodiments that weigh down our abilities to see with any clarity, let alone any empathy. Who are we? All these artists attempt to visualize this problem in new ways.

***

Steyerl understands why we run from images, from the visual, particularly now:

> Their instincts (and their intelligence) tell them that photographic or moving images are dangerous devices of capture: of time, affect, productive forces,

and subjectivity. They can jail you or shame you forever; they can trap you in hardware monopolies and conversion conundrums, and, moreover, once these images are online they will never be deleted again.[33]

The problem is not just technology, however, as this chapter has outlined, although technology really doesn't help. Images do jail us, they shame us, they make us incapable of knowing ourselves and everyone else. To put it another way, as Springsteen so eloquently sings, he wants to know "what it feels like in the back of your pink Cadillac." The song is upbeat and sexy, but the underlying message is about wanting understanding, a connection. In the song this wanting is a wish, a wondering, never realized. And it is corporeal, it's about feeling what it is like to be another person. That longing—perhaps more than the hoped-for knowledge—is the drive of the speaker's deepest desire.

What does it feel like? If only I could see you, maybe I would know who you are.

4

WHEN

Provocation

It was supposed to be a very big deal, globally speaking. The European Commission, European Research Council, and the Event Horizon Telescope (EHT) project issued a teaser press release on April 1, 2019, to get everyone ready for what they promised would be "groundbreaking" news. The big reveal of "the first direct visual evidence of a supermassive black hole and its shadow" came ten days later in a massive global announcement, including research papers, graphics, packaged quotes, and a webpage all designed to ensure that the exciting information was kept in proper scientific context as it was breathlessly reported all over the world.[1] The image was front-page news for many international newspapers, blasted across television and the internet, and was seemingly everywhere within minutes of its release.

The impact, however, was not what had been expected. There was no collective awe, but instead what was best described as a decidedly "been there, done that" nonchalance. The whole thing was fodder for the jokes of late-night talk show hosts by the following week.

The black hole that was visualized sits at the center of Messier 87, a galaxy 55 million light years from earth.

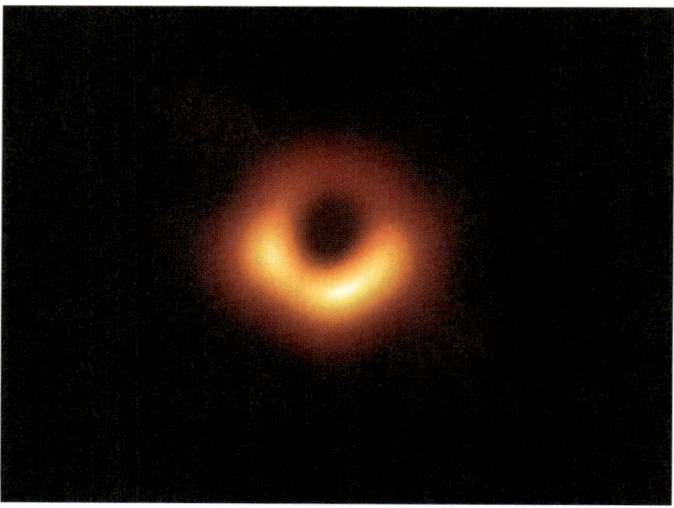

Figure 16 "First Image of a Black Hole," April 10, 2019. Credit: EHT Collaboration.

The hole is too far for any earthbound lens or even one mounted on extant spacecraft to capture a picture of it in any conventional sense. Then how did we come to see this "direct visual evidence"? The source and nature of the image were described in multiple ways in the announcement, including the aforementioned term "direct visual evidence." It was also called a "picture," the product of "multiple calibration and imaging methods," an "observed image," "interferometry," "observations," "results," a "shadow," and "a new window." If this seems confusing, or strangely imprecise for a scientific team, it signaled that the creation of the image itself was a complex undertaking. Part of a multiyear, multi-institutional, and multitelescope project, the image is a composite of datasets of multiple origins processed to appear as a singular, cohesive image, or, more specifically, to look like a photograph. It is, however, definitely *not* a photograph, although that distinction was lost in many of the retellings, descriptions, and commentary surrounding the discovery and its imaging.

Which is to say that the image was nothing like the iconic pictures of space created in the past. Take, for instance, the image of Buzz Aldrin on the moon captured in 1969 by fellow astronaut Neil Armstrong with a Hasselblad 500E camera. That 1969 flight was the first to include several different photographic devices in order to record the American space program's moment of triumph. Perhaps most important among them was the film camera,

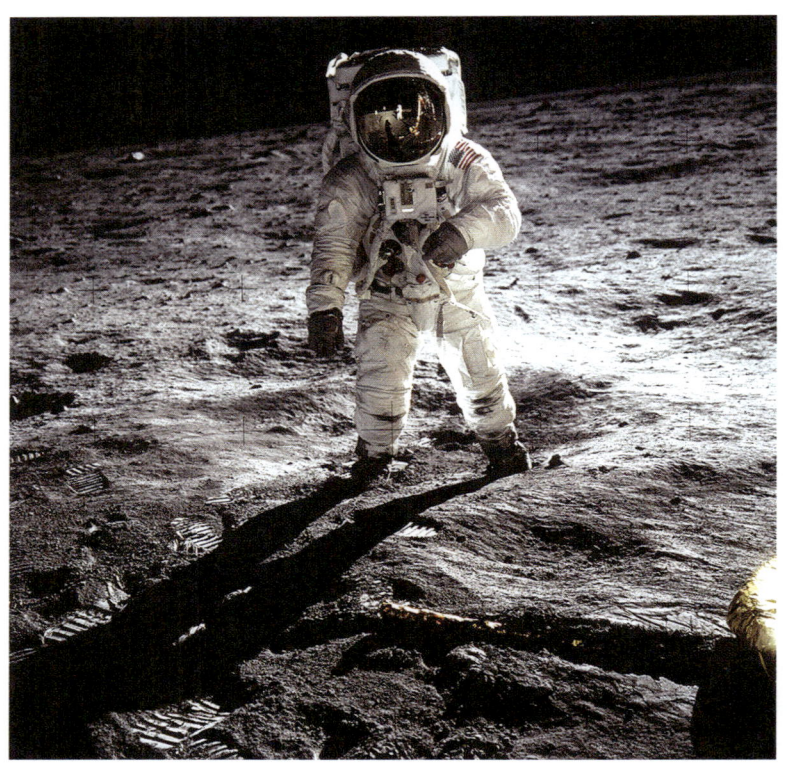

Figure 17 Neil Armstrong, *Astronaut Buzz Aldrin, Lunar Module Pilot, Walks on the Surface of the Moon Near the Leg of the Lunar Module (LM) "Eagle" During the Apollo 11 Extravehicular Activity (EVA)*, 1969. Photo credit: NASA.

used to capture and then televise images of the first man stepping onto the moon and planting an American flag. A few years later, in 1972, the iconic "Blue Marble" shot of planet Earth was taken by the crew of Apollo 17, providing the first image of the whole planet surrounded by space. This view provided an image that Nicholas Mirzoeff notes made the planet "at once immense and knowable."[2] In short, humanity went from centuries of hand-rendered images of space to the ability to create and consider it in photographs.

This visual and technological transition radically shifted depictions of outer space. A rich visual culture involving space and the moon predated the Apollo missions by centuries.[3] Imaginations of the extraterrestrial have been a global visual preoccupation. Humanity's earliest notions of space mimicked life on Earth, with plants, animals, and humans populating the stars. People bent the heavens to make space seem more familiar, more like home. In the early modern period, Chinese sky maps were marked with animals; European celestial maps used animals and humans to form constellations; and Abd al-Rahman ibn 'Umar al-Sufi's *Book of the Constellations of the Fixed Stars* (964) used illustrations to help cohere what was known about space. These visuals mapped a sky that reminded people of earth and made what was far away visually accessible.

Shifting global knowledge about science, changes in religious conceptions of Earth, and expanded aesthetic options opened with increased globalization. This was manifested in imagery that even in the mid-twentieth century featured a wide array of visual motifs to represent what was known about outer space. Even planetariums, sites devoted to producing and making believable knowledge about space, often did not worry about the differences, placing cutting-edge illustrations of the moon as seen through telescopes next to artistically rendered astrological signs, which could be next to popular and commercial imagery depicting a fantastic future of space travel and colonization. The visual culture of space could be exacting and deeply embedded in physics and mathematical principles, but the long premodern visual history of space was allowed to sit side by side with newer knowledge.

The photographs and films of the 1960s and 1970s radically shifted this dynamic. Placing primacy on visual accuracy and the "real," these filmic images from extraterrestrial perspectives almost immediately supplanted all other modes of visual production in regard to scientific education. This was starkly displayed in 2000 when the American Museum of Natural History in New York opened its newly reconceptualized Rose Center for Earth and Space (the former Hayden Planetarium), which featured *only* photographic and digital images on its newly bare white walls; all other hand-rendered visual objects were evacuated to scientists' offices or the archives. Out went the astrological signs and murals of Indigenous stories about the moon, and in came screens full of NASA-fed imagery.

Yet, while images that approximated photographs (explanation to come in short order) came to dominate scientific spaces and dialogues, other kinds of space imagery proliferated in spite of these new technologies. In 1977 the first installment of the cinematic space epic *Star Wars* was released, a film that was itself in dialogue with the 1968 Stanley Kubrick film *2001: A Space Odyssey*, which had in turn been inspired by Japanese *tokusatsu* films of the 1950s that commonly featured outer space and alien beings. If scientific communities were becoming more precise in their imagery and concerned with reinforcing notions of veracity through the visual vocabulary of photography, popular visual culture was taking viewers across galaxies and the farthest reaches of what film and narrative could imagine. Saloons on faraway planets packed with diverse aliens and a sprinkling of humans competed with photographs and museum exhibits of moon rocks.

Just as technology made taking photographs from near space possible, it almost immediately ran into a roadblock. Space is really big, and everything else is very far away from Earth and its immediate surroundings. New forms and technologies of seeing were needed.

What evolved was the hybrid imagery suggested in the language of the black hole press release. Data must be *turned* into an image. As data, it has no discernable visual structure that can be appreciated by the human eye. What emerged has been described by scholar Lisa Messeri as "place-making practices," which is to say various strategies for making data, calibrating information based on extant visual knowledge, processing multiple views and data points, editing that information, discarding data that doesn't fit the shape taking form, mostly by tossing the outliers, and pulling all of that together into a visual representation that is recognizable.

This is tricky when trying to visualize planets, for example, but it is even more complex when attempting to visualize a black hole, given that its very nature is marked by its invisibility. All neighboring light is sucked into a black hole; none can escape to reach our eyes or cameras. What scientists sought was "to capture an image of the hot, glowing gas falling into a black hole."[4] Thus, to show us the black hole, the scientists had to locate and then depict what was mostly unseeable at the precise moment when superheated gas was "falling into" it.

A known black hole closer to Earth wasn't ideal in terms of data access, so this daunting challenge was made even more complicated by the need to use a more distant black hole for the case study. To acquire the data, it was then necessary to coordinate eight telescopes at several points around the globe for four days. This is how NASA explained the process of data gathering and processing:

As each telescope acquired data from the target black hole, the digitized data and time stamp were recorded on computer disk media. Gathering data for four days around the world gave the team a substantial amount of data to process. The recorded media were then physically transported to a central location because the amount of data, around 5 petabytes, exceeds what the current internet speeds can handle. At this central location, data from all eight sites were synchronized using the time stamps and combined to create a composite set of images, revealing the never-before-seen silhouette of M87*'s event horizon.[5]

Yet even the EHT team needed to clarify that this was only a partial image despite the tremendous quantity of data they'd compiled. To compensate for this lack, team programmers developed "imaging algorithms" designed to "fill in the gaps of data." To clarify this for the general public, EHT used the metaphor of playing on a piano with broken keys; the song might not always sound right but you can pick out the tune. To bring home the point, EHT provided an audio example using the 1990 Vanilla Ice hit single "Ice, Ice Baby." After starting with what sounds like a random string of notes, they come together in a recognizable if not exact version of the familiar song. Noting that it is pretty amazing that "your brain can fill in the holes," the spokesperson explained that imaging algorithms basically do the same thing—they fill in the holes.[6] Incomplete data is crafted into what the project believes is the most reasonable assemblage to make the picture of the black hole. This way of seeing—which is driven by machines and algorithms—is not just how black holes are visualized; it is how much of the visual data and knowledge we encounter daily are created. Space is made out of numbers, time, and computer-generated conjectures.

The look of the photograph is likewise noteworthy. Presumably all kinds of visual techniques could have been used, but since the language of photography and the digital have dominated visual culture and questions of facticity since post-1970s space exploration, it was photographic referents to which they turned to "fill in the holes." The result is not a photograph in any physical or historical sense. Instead, the picture of the black hole is a simulation of data made to look like a photograph. Photographs have come to express authenticity as science, reality, and truth; even with all we know about how they have always been manipulated, they still clearly have particular visual currency.

The image was meant to inspire, reassure, instill wonder, and educate, but the immediate reaction from the world of the internet was snarky. Twitter and Instagram filled with pithy notes about being unimpressed with the visual, noting that it seemed to lack inspirational quality.

Others noted the black hole's uncanny resemblance to the Eye of Sauron as depicted in Peter Jackson's film adaptation of the *Lord of the Rings* trilogy. The overwhelming impression of the image was that many had seen it before. Which, of course, they had.

EHT's explanation through music resonated with this feeling. "Ice, Ice Baby" has a beat borrowed from Queen and David Bowie, who in turn were broadly borrowing from a myriad of musical influences. We *had* heard it before, just as we have seen the black hole before. We know the stuff "filling" in the holes. It's the same stuff the creators of the image know. Messeri describes observing a team of geologists as they developed maps of different planetary geographies—they spent their evenings watching sci-fi films.[7]

So what exactly are we looking at when we see this new image of a black hole? Are we seeing what is really out there, or only what we (and our computers) are already capable of imagining?

When will we get there?

One of the most frequent clichés animating calls to action is: If not now, when? *When* is an interesting word. It doesn't always demand, or even imagine, a future, and it may very well point to the past. Either way, however, *when* is always firmly rooted in the present—from this point in time, when did or will we leave? When did or will you do something? When did or will I finally understand?

In some instances, the visual response to "When?" is "Now!" In others, it is "Well, then."

This chapter considers the visual *when* and its possibilities, which means we will simultaneously be examining visual vocabularies of the *now*: in other words, how we *visually* locate ourselves in regard to time. Time and space have been visually collapsed historically and across cultures. This is evidenced in visuals as diverse as the imagery of the black hole (which is a phenomenon of time and space) and various kinds of Indigenous maps that are rooted in space/time grids.[8] The modern natural history diorama which features taxidermied animals and painted landscapes similarly suggests the way in which time and nature are entangled visually.[9] When, in other words, is often mixed up into where, but for our purposes it is more generative to focus on the visual *when*.

Perhaps no aspect of contemporary visual culture is more concerned with *when* and its relation to the *now* than images devoted to the diverse ways humanity locates itself and its place, and cares for or devours the resources of earth and space. It is a visual culture of urgency, dread, hope, and regret, because it has come to focus so intently on the visual record of global warming and climate change and grappling with the potential devastations of the future.

"When?" always carries a tinge of the existential—for every person, definitely sometime—but the visual cultures of climate crisis address the question collectively to humanity, looking not to mere death but to extinction.

In the novelist Amitav Ghosh's 2016 book *The Great Derangement*, he seeks to address why artists, such as himself, can't seem to get their heads and imaginations around the growing climate crisis. He is unrelenting in his assessment that this is not merely some unfortunate omission, but potentially the very heart of the reason for the global human community's feeble attempts to change habits and actions, or to address the growing evidence that we are destroying our planet. Ghosh sees a great deal of blame to be shared all around, but argues ultimately that "when future generations look back upon the Great Derangement they will certainly blame the leaders and politicians of the time for their failure to address the climate crisis. But they may well hold artists and writers to be equally culpable—for the imagining of possibilities is not, after all, the job of politicians and bureaucrats."[10]

It is literally a crisis of vision. Ghosh demands that we consider how visual culture has failed to show us the problem and the stakes, how it has failed to make us see. He points to the terrible consequences: because we don't see the emergency, we fail to address it. To think on this in another way, what might be shown, and how would that make the world see? Clearly, the tragic animated scene of a sad-eyed polar bear unable to climb up onto a shrinking ice float from former Vice-President Al Gore's documentary *An Inconvenient Truth* didn't do the job. The answer to "When?" clearly isn't 2006.[11]

It is important here to clarify the "we" and "us" in the story of climate change. Often in dialogues about the environment there is a tendency to obscure culpability or disperse blame within general narratives of possibility and progress: "We all got in this mess, how are we going to fix it?"[12] On the other hand, there are clearly identifiable segments of the global population who will bear an outsized burden from the violent consequences of climate change—who already are. To combine those who have disproportionately profited and those who have and will disproportionately suffer as if they share blame or costs performs another cruel and unjust erasure. Industrial nations, corporate capitalism, and the elite and middle classes in Europe and the United States bear the majority of the responsibility, and have also crafted the rhetorical, political, and economic paradigms that justify emerging economies and new world powers in exacerbating these problems. It is the world's poor and formerly colonized of the Global South who suffer first and most, again.

This brings "us" to another bit of controversy "we" need to confront: When, exactly, are we? Some have come to think of this period—this *when*—as the Anthropocene. First posited by geologists, the term names a new epoch in the earth's geologic time during which the impact of humans is so significant as to be the dominant factor shaping and changing every ecosystem, the land, the sea, the planet's atmosphere; no aspect of life on Earth remains untouched by human actions. This time is different, necessitating, some argue, the designation of a new epoch. Almost as controversial as the suggestion of a new epoch is the identification of when it could be said to have started. Suggestions range from the spread of human agriculture (about 8,000 years ago) to the steam engine (1712) and the first nuclear detonation (1945).

Proponents of the Anthropocene designation have met with significant backlash. Much of it revolves around the charge of anthropocentrism or human arrogance in some form. Many have convincingly argued that the term works to naturalize human superiority and privilege human behaviors, or that it does not address the epic imbalance among humans in terms of responsibility for the changes. Thus, whereas scholars like Dipesh Chakrabarty find the Anthropocene to be a politically and ideologically useful term, others such as Gayatri Spivak and Bruno Latour have made convincing and urgent use of the term "planetary" instead to focus on the need to *rethink* and *recreate* (rather than simply rename) senses of time, place, and relationships among and within species and environments.[13]

Acts of seeing and not seeing, erasure, and imagination are at the very heart of climate change narratives, as is that inevitable question, "When?" Ghosh's accusation is also a call to action. When will humanity be motivated by what we see or are shown? Mirzoeff argues that "the first step is to recognize how deeply embedded in our very sensorium and modern ways of seeing the Anthropocene-aesthetic-capitalist complex of modern visuality has become."[14] The scholar Donna Haraway puts it differently: "[the] eye fucks the world to make-techno-monsters."[15] Is the eye the way to un-fuck it?

The visual realm has, in fact, been an incredibly, even devastatingly effective tool for shaping people's understandings of the environment, their pleasures in it, and their threats and obligations to it. Anyone here scared to go in the water because of sharks? Got a visual on that? What we know of the natural world is bound up, for better or worse, with visual culture.

In order to consider carefully our inherited stories about the earth and the things that live on it, Haraway argues that we must "stay with the trouble." This means resisting the compulsion to look away, but also inhabiting trouble, being in it, making it, and healing it *now*, in the present, not *when*. Haraway calls us to "stir up potent response(s) to devastating events, as well as to settle troubled waters and rebuild quiet places."[16] This is a tall order, and as we have seen in previous chapters, a lot of images stand in the way. Yet a productive visual culture, one that inspires action, attention, and being in the *now*, Ghosh

The visual realm has been an incredibly effective tool for shaping people's understandings of the environment, their pleasures in it, and their threats and obligations to it.

begs us to understand, is also possible and imperative. As always, visual culture is both problem and solution to figuring out *when*.

When not where

Often, when a visual image appears to be about geography or the land, it is in fact about something else entirely: time, mobility, freedom, fear. In 2016, @streetview.portraits began posting Google Street View images on Instagram. The views were from all over the world, not of highly trafficked tourist spots but of random streets and lone houses; sometimes they featured people but never crowds. A sense of isolation dominates the tone of the images, as does a notable attention to space: space to spread out, space to breathe, space to look around. Artist Jacqui Kenny, who posted these images, identifies herself as agoraphobic, making her unable to physically travel to any of the locations she captures in her images. She describes her process:

> I found a surprising and unique refuge in the creative possibilities of Google Street View. I began clicking through Google Maps to navigate to faraway countries like Mongolia, Senegal, and Chile. I found remote towns and dusty landscapes, vibrant

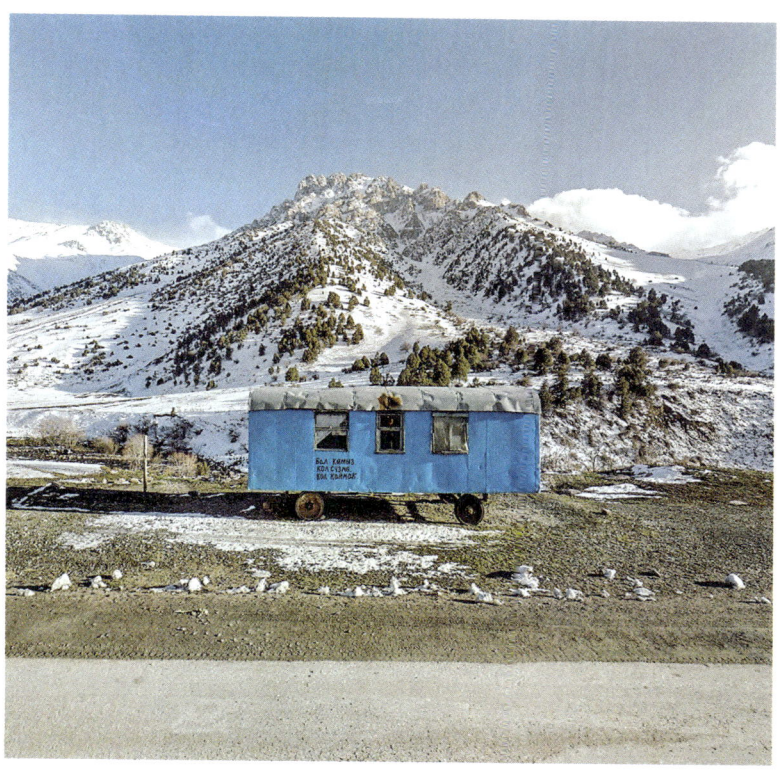

Figure 18 Jacqui Kenny, *Mobile Home: Kyrgyzstan*, 2017. Photograph, Instagram @streetview.portraits. Image courtesy of the artist, created by Jacqui Kenny. Copyright Google.

architectural gems, and anonymous people, all frozen in time. I was intrigued by the strange and expansive parallel universe of Street View, and took screen shots to capture and preserve its hidden, magical realms.[17]

Travel and the opportunity to see new things, places, and people necessarily generate new ways of thinking about oneself and one's relationship to the world. It is a great luxury that remains unavailable to many. More than this, Kenny's work suggests, it is a luxury constrained by ability. People with disabilities have always struggled in diverse ways to move through space and beyond confines. Travel can be about getting outside oneself, escaping the body; unless, of course, you can't.

Online technology has revolutionized travel in many ways, further blurring the "when" and the "where." Google Maps and Street View and similar applications allow for all kinds of visualizations that were not possible just a decade ago. Admittedly there are limits, which Kenny feels acutely: "I'll see something in the distance that looks amazing, but then the car stops or something gets in the way. It happens ninety per cent of the time. I always have to be prepared for that disappointment."[18] All travel has its disappointments, many of which emerge from sight's limitations and the places eyes just cannot go or cannot see. In that sense, Kenny's project is very much the same as those of travel photographers who physically go to the locations they depict, or of tourists. All crave better angles or want to get a closer look, but find some things impossible. We want access to everything, and the frustrations of denial are as sharp on Google Street View as they are in person.

But even when we have access, what exactly are we able to see of the environment, its inhabitants, or the planet? Kenny's work is amazing, yet in her posts a distinct version of the world with a specific tone, color, and sightline emerges. Distinctive ways of seeing are inevitably guided by the dominant stories and visual narratives of one's culture and time. Kenny is no exception: her "hidden, magical realms" within Google Street View are not new discoveries but familiar scenes constructed several times over.

The landscape as an idea is itself a strategic tool and visual argument about space and time that relies on repeating or disrupting common tropes in order to be seen and understood. This sense of the recognizable provides steady location for the viewer. When people don't have a sense of their body's place or orientation in space, they struggle with what Messeri calls "intangible modes of being."[19] They literally fear losing themselves. The brain tries to sort through the chaos of sensory data, giving it order and legibility. In the process, the moment and place move from the "perceived to the experienced."[20] This is also an apt description of the creation of landscape imagery. Not all information can hold the same visual significance, some details must be highlighted and others ignored, some things are rearranged. These visual arrangements again are as much about time, or the when, as they are about any specific geography. Looking at the land or the sky is often about looking to see something else entirely.

Take, for example, *Evening Bell from Mist-Shrouded Temple* and *Autumn Moon over Lake Dongting*, paired painted scrolls from the mid to late fifteenth century. They are painted in the style of An Gyeon, one of the most important Korean artists of the Joseon Dynasty, and were likely part of an eight-scroll series of scenes depicting the land around the Xiao and Xiang rivers in Hunan, China. For Chinese artists, this had been a popular and commonly reproduced landscape since the eleventh century. The fact that this piece was made by a Korean artist testifies to the tastes of the Korean court and the preferences both aesthetic and intellectual of the period.

Both scrolls are vague on the specific geography of the Chinese location. This is in keeping with the aesthetic belief of the time that those kinds of details were not meaningful to the artist or viewers. Instead, the grand mountains, elegant and graceful trees, and moonless sky were the scrolls' visual markers of what the landscape meant and what was worth seeing.[21]

People and the built environment are depicted in a way that melts all evidence of their existence into the scene. Rooftops are visible but do not clash with or disrupt

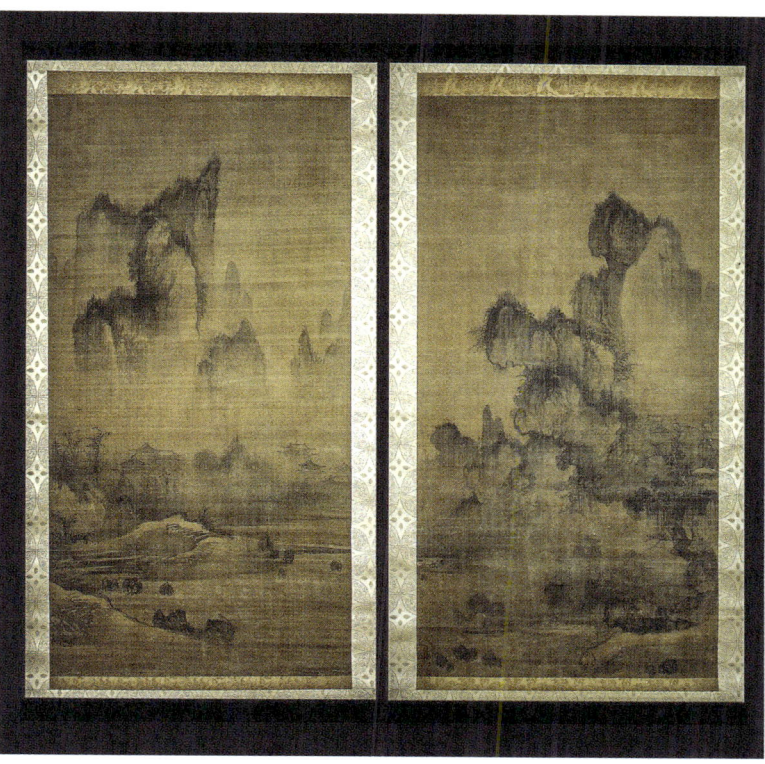

Figure 19 Style of An Gyeon, *Evening Bell from Mist-Shrouded Temple* and *Autumn Moon over Lake Dongting*, ca. 1450–1500. Pair of hanging scrolls; ink on silk, each scroll 35⅜ × 17⅞ in. Metropolitan Museum of Art, New York.

natural surroundings; curved temples organically meld with the brush lines that surround them. The artist thus urges viewers to see that nature, humanity, and spirituality seamlessly fit together in a singular whole.

This notion of the organic connections between humans and nature in comfortable intimacy and mutuality would become somewhat familiar to landscape imagery in Europe and North America as well as East Asia. Even in eighteenth-century romantic landscape painting with its emphasis on nature's harshness and dangers, depicted in scenes with violent thunderstorms, devastated trees, or desolate fog, nature still attends to human needs. The visual sublime was ultimately about communicating lessons of *gravitas* and how to feel one's body and spirit in profound ways. It is not altogether ridiculous to draw a direct visual line from the Korean scrolls of the fifteenth century to eighteenth-century romantic landscape and through to contemporary television and print media images advertising pickup trucks with a backdrop of majestic mountains. Our eyes have been trained to see the earth not as itself but as something else: as a feeling, as time, as a sensation.

Which brings us back to Kenny's works on Instagram. We should not underestimate the sense of freedom, creative possibility, and fundamental joy Kenny demonstrates in her work of visual place-making through Google Street View. Indeed, the artistic use of landscapes personally unseen, as in the Korean scroll example, has a long history. But we must also ask, are Google Street View and Google Earth free of symbols and embedded meanings? Is Kenny's source material benign? What codes, knowledge, and prejudices come with those images?

To start teasing apart this set of questions, we must first consider how the images are made. Google Earth, like most satellite-produced mapping imagery, comes from military technology. Take, for instance, an image of the Venetian lagoon. It is easy to focus on the details, the inlets, the land, the contrasting colors (all simulated), or to take in the coastline as a whole. One might think of it not as a map, but a design comprised of line and color.

The technology is easy and useful and so commonplace now that we might forget it wasn't initially generated for tourists, or for the curious internet searcher. It was made with the very specific goal of looking at other countries, marking changes, movements, and differences for both defensive and offensive military advantage. According to scholar T. J. Demos, it is therefore "embedded in a specific political and economic framework, comprising a visual system delivered and constituted by the post-Cold War and largely Western-based military-state-corporate apparatus."[22] The tool of general vision has been constructed to meet a very specific use, and it is worth questioning whether that intended function every really dissipates from the visual objects the tool presents. What Kenny, for example, sees as the limits of her view are perhaps far less

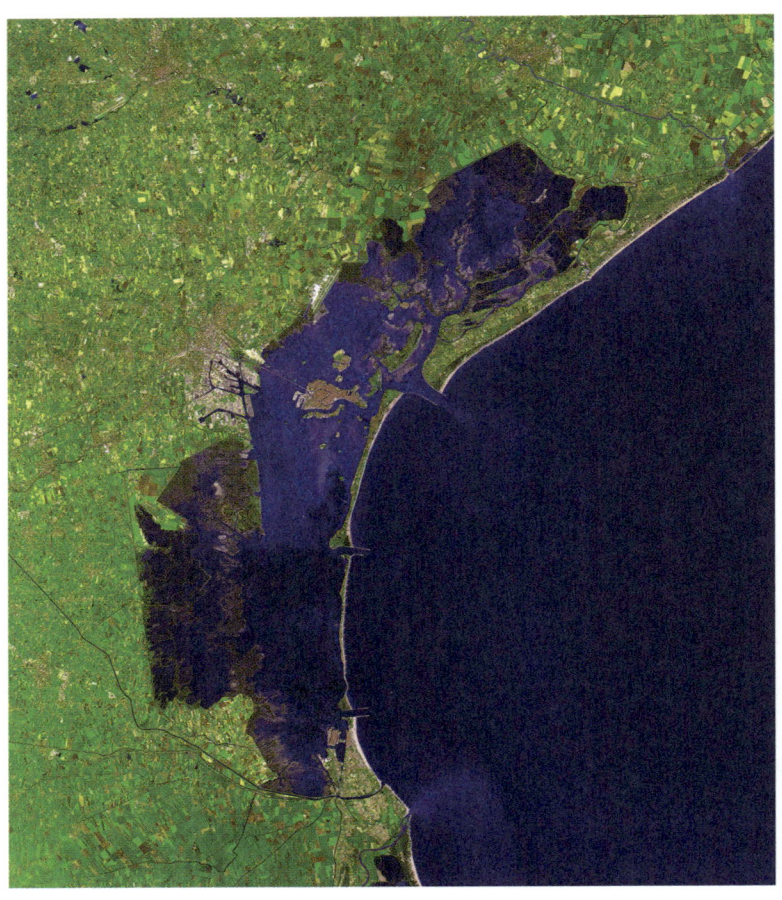

Figure 20 Venetian lagoon, taken by Advanced Spaceborne Thermal Emission and Reflection Radiometer, an imaging instrument flying on Terra, a NASA satellite, acquired on December 9, 2001 (simulated natural color). Photo credit: NASA/GSFC/MITI/ERSDAC/JAROS, and U.S./Japan ASTER Science Team.

benign or accidental, manufactured rather by what outgoing US president and former general Dwight Eisenhower once called the "military-industrial-complex."

More insidious is the possibility that technology is permanently inhibiting our ability to orient ourselves without our phones and dashboard screens. Global positioning systems (GPSs) were also developed for military uses, specifically to aid in guiding missiles to their targets. Currently there are more than 5 billion GPS platforms at work in the world; the one probably closest to you is in your phone. GPS promises not only to reproduce a map of roads and landmarks in an easy-to-read format, but to assess the fastest or most direct way for one to move from point A to point B. It can tell us the distance, the gas stations on the way, figure out how much traffic will slow one down and for how long, and even visually show which would be faster, walking or taking public transportation. There is even a thing called "death by GPS" where people who don't have a sense of their actual surroundings instead rely on GPS and find themselves in a lake or over a gorge. This isn't really all that surprising, as there is growing evidence that these digitally constructed maps are shifting human internal spatial sensibilities. Again, we find visual culture's shifting technologies and perceptions changing the relationship between the body and the space around it. Author Greg Milner cautions that "there is an enormous value in knowing the exact placement of things in physical space."²³ We might lose ourselves entirely, to put it another way.

What has changed in the twenty-first century is the authority of digital images, GPS, and Google Street View. Like the image of the black hole, an increasing number of pictures that we see, that seem like very good and precise photographs of data, are not photographs at all. They are illustrations, imaginations, and reconfigurations of information. If we knew this, we might trust them as much as viewers of the *Evening Bell from Mist-Shrouded Temple* and *Autumn Moon over Lake Dongting* trusted those scrolls as accurate depictions of the topography of China. The scrolls' value and their truth lay elsewhere. They were still sources of information and instruction about what the land meant then. Audiences understood the visual exchange and dialogue for what it was, not about the land but about ideas.

Contemporary visual culture messes considerably with the dynamic by which landscape images represent some concrete truth or authority about the land. This is why it is helpful to consider digital scholar Wendy Hui Kyong Chun's wise reminder, "what form of agency does not require risk?"²⁴ These new images have value, but we need to consider the value thoughtfully. Historically, there has been a human (even if an unknown person), some being with agency, at the heart of each visual object who can offer (hopefully) some broad philosophical sense to engage with. "I hate Picasso" is a legitimate thought because there is a Picasso to hate. But with algorithm generators, best guesses, data synthesis, computer-to-computer visualization, there is no there there. This is what frightens many about the future of visual culture: that there will be no person directly, immediately, or really ever at the helm.

After sociologist Janet Vertesi spent time with the teams that employed the latest tools to visualize the planet Mars, she suggested there might be a better, more realistic way to see Mars and other space bodies. We should "see like a Rover," she concludes. Vertesi refers here to NASA's Mars Exploration Rover mission that sent two robotic vehicles to the planet in 2004; one collected data until 2010 while the other was operational until 2018. Rather than accepting the ways of seeing authorized by the state, which are narrow and made to seem more coherent than the actual data allows, Vertesi describes seeing like a Rover as a process that "enroll(s) multiple observers in complex social relations, but these relations are oriented toward consensus, not authoritarian control."[25] The technology may still carry the traces of its original uses and modes of seeing and not seeing, but an intentional process of collaborative and diverse reuse aimed at multiplicity rather than the illusion of a singular truth will facilitate better seeing and richer knowledge.

Scholar Joanna Zylinska takes another equally encouraging position, arguing that we should rethink this imagery as nonhuman photography. This "conjoined human-nonhuman agency and vision . . . thus functions as both a form of control and a life-shaping force."[26] We needn't fear nonhuman visual products, she writes, or worry too much about their origin story. Control has always been a part of the equation; always a part of the earth's many visualizations. Control is the human part, which nonhuman imagery might just shake us free of. Zylinska sees a bright human future in such a move, with nonhuman eyes allowing us to finally see clearly the world that surrounds us. She argues this new vision will "allow humans to see beyond the humanist limitations of their current philosophies and world views, to unsee themselves in their godlike positioning of both everywhere and nowhere, and to become reanchored and reattached again."[27] Of course, one might ask, when were "we" so anchored and attached?

If not now . . .

Visually speaking, the picture doesn't really look like much. Mostly white ice and snow, with a gentle ombré on the horizon line that moves the color from white to a rich sky blue. The zigzag rupture does not look that ominous on its face. It could be the track of some motorized vehicle, some crooked path from one place to the next. You could even be forgiven for imagining it was made by a dog sled. In the left corner of the frame hangs a plane's wing and engines, anchoring the viewer firmly inside the plane, looking out a window.

Scholar Alex Bush describes this image differently: "I found myself unable to bear witness to the rupture in Larsen-C" as it is "too horrifying to contemplate." It is "seeing the death of the entire earth, and all its inhabitants, in advance."[28] The key to Bush's distress is the mention of "Larsen-C," which designates an ice shelf in the Antarctic. These shelves have been monitored by scientists with

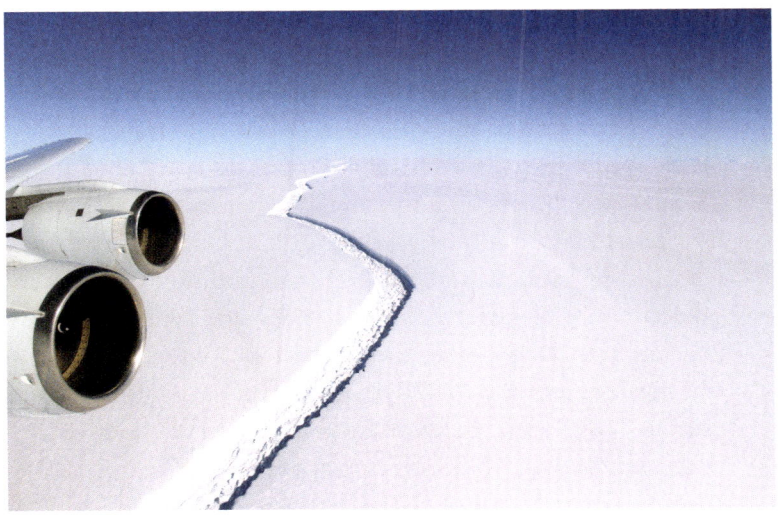

Figure 21 Rift in Larsen C from the vantage point of NASA's DC-8 research aircraft, November 10, 2016. Photo: John Sonntag, NASA.

increasing anxiety, as global warming has already caused several of them to break apart, suggesting a start to the fundamental reshaping of the planet. While Larsen C had already lost several parts, in 2016 a far more significant rift was identified, first in satellite imagery, then, when weather permitted, by direct visual confirmation. This photograph is evidence of that confirmation. The line is definitely not tracks in the snow; it might be the beginning of the end of humanity and most other life on earth. For Bush, this photo is the end of the world as we know it—a mass death foretold, a horror show. It is a photograph that cannot be looked at because it is a picture of *when*, and the deadline has passed.

Film studies scholar E. Ann Kaplan might wonder whether what Bush is speaking of here is "Pretraumatic Stress Syndrome" (PreTSS), wherein trauma is suffered in advance of a climate apocalypse. Film viewers and fiction fans see climate annihilation coming and they are already damaged by it. Kaplan suggests this condition is a major preoccupation in contemporary literary and film output. Readers and filmgoers are being fed repeated images of climate disasters and their dystopian outcomes.[29] Besides science's "real" images, there is no end to made-up ones that can play out all our worst nightmares.

A recent example would be *Mad Max: Fury Road*, the 2015 movie directed by George Miller. A reimagining of the trilogy from the late 1970s and 1980s (also directed by Miller), *Fury Road* takes on a far more urgent tone and political resonance. A reboot of sorts, the 2015 film begins by suggesting that this global collapse was not generic but specifically environmental. Because of oil, avarice, and abuse of the land, future Earth is a dry, desolate desert, where there is no vegetation, all the animals have been twisted and deformed so as to be nearly unrecognizable, and human life is defined by water scarcity, violence, strong-man domination, and physical disability and illness. This future is also, inexplicably, almost entirely populated by white people.[30]

This is not the only recent apocalyptic narrative, visual and otherwise, that posits civilization's end and a violent future in which only the strongest and whitest will survive. What these films also visualize, aside from overwhelming racism, is the impossibly narcissistic individual opportunity to start over, meaning that the same bodies that held power and visibility in the old world and are largely to blame for the state of the new one will get another bite at the apple. While fear and dread inspire flights of horrific fantasy, these versions of the future often only further reinforce the social injustices and desires of the present. Projecting into the future what the earth will look like serves to ease the audience of now. The visual representation is of the land, burnt and destroyed, but the message is about time and power, a salve for the current inaction or trauma at what has been unleashed.

This is exactly the opposite of what Ghosh says we need. This is the kind of art, the kind of imagination that pulls us back into ourselves, not outward to collective action, and certainly not to *when*. As scholar Rob Nixon asks, "How can we convert into image and narrative the disasters that are slow moving and long in the making, disasters that are anonymous and that star nobody?"[31]

So we return to Larsen C, and to documentary film, satellite imagery, illustration, charts, memes, computer simulations, endless visuals created by human and nonhuman alike. The fact is, there is already a robust visual culture of ways to see the evidence of what is happening to the planet. Graphics and countless charts and clusters arrange and rearrange data and beg for eyes and action. Much time, attention, and talent are invested in creating the right collage of imagery that will shake humanity from its global stupor and incite action.

Yet, as Bush's response to the ruptured Antarctic ice shelf image suggests, images can backfire, making things appear too desperate, too sad, too hopeless. We look away instead of confronting our when. The documentary and factual might falter, but other makers have imagined ways to resee the world and its environments. Contemporary artist Valerie Hegarty looks back to august Western landscape history to grab the viewer's attention and emotion in order to generate new sight and new action. Describing her work *Warped Landscape* (2016), the artist writes:

[It] is a ceramic work that continues my interest with appropriating iconic images from American History and altering them in ways that critique their content. I painted the landscape with underglaze as a loose and diminutive copy of Albert Bierstadt's *Among the Sierras* from 1868—the original a heroically scaled sweeping view of pristine and abundant western woodlands. Part fact and part fiction, it was these idealized landscapes—also devoid of Indigenous peoples—that helped strengthen the idea of manifest destiny, that America was the "Promised Land" encouraging European settlers to push westward. The crumpling of the work refers to the gesture of the artist that has made a failed image. The rendering of the image and crumpling in ceramic concretizes the failure of the American myth to reflect the brutal reality of the violence wrought in the name of expansionism and industrialization, including the decimation of indigenous peoples and the destruction of the landscape itself.[32]

Hegarty's piece is a bit like a hidden explosive in regard to seeing the land and the legacy of seeing. The material itself, ceramic, has a very complex history within the categories of fine art. In some cultures, ceramics are highly valued, but in Western art they have generally been deemed decorative, thus not really art. That Hegarty works in this

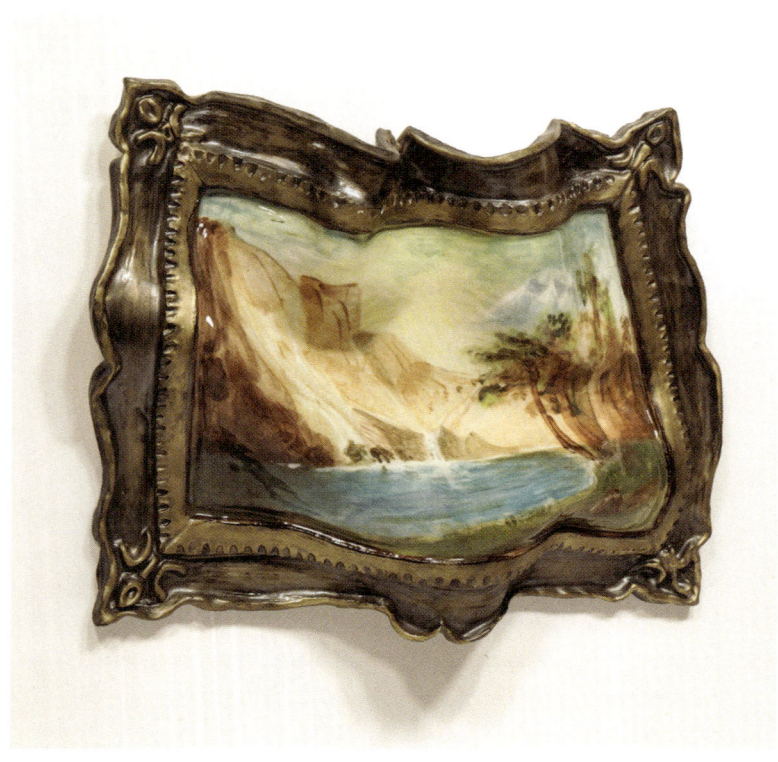

Figure 22 Valerie Hegarty, *Warped Landscape*, 2016. Glazed ceramic, 11 × 13 × 3 in. Image courtesy of the artist.

material has a decidedly gendered and racial context: the very bodies and materials left out of some dialogues about land and visualization will be edged back in, even by her choice of the material to use.

She is also confronting one of the most famous and collected of American landscape artists, whose works have come to define a particular aesthetic of the American West. Bierstadt, an artist originally from Germany, produced images of the western territories after the Civil War and visually redirected a conversation from the trials of war and race to what he depicted as an open and opportunity-filled frontier. This land, as Hegarty notes, was already occupied by Indigenous peoples; indeed, when Bierstadt was painting his majestic views of a naturally optimistic and open land, the US federal government was warring with numerous tribes, forcing them to relocate, and negating or simply ignoring treaties. In short, this was a period of slaughter and sorrow across much of the West, but that's not what Bierstadt and other white landscape artists of the time depicted. Their imagery was about victory, conquest, and the rich, ever-expansive lands that awaited white settlers and tourists.

Hegarty literally curdles this visual dialogue, twisting Bierstadt's image so that it is still recognizable but forever altered. She argues that before we can move forward, we must intervene in the past. We must disassemble what has been made of the land and its meanings and make it into something new. We've seen this kind of reclamation before; Mickalene Thomas, for example, is doing similar work with the legacy of black women's bodies in visual culture. Both artists charge that it is not enough to simply pivot to "new" imagery. Nothing can be new without dismantling the visual past. Thus, as Thomas attempts to visually recreate a "who," Hegarty pulls in the "when" of how we look now.

Korean artist Han Seok Hyun moves at the question of landscape, visual activism, and environmental change

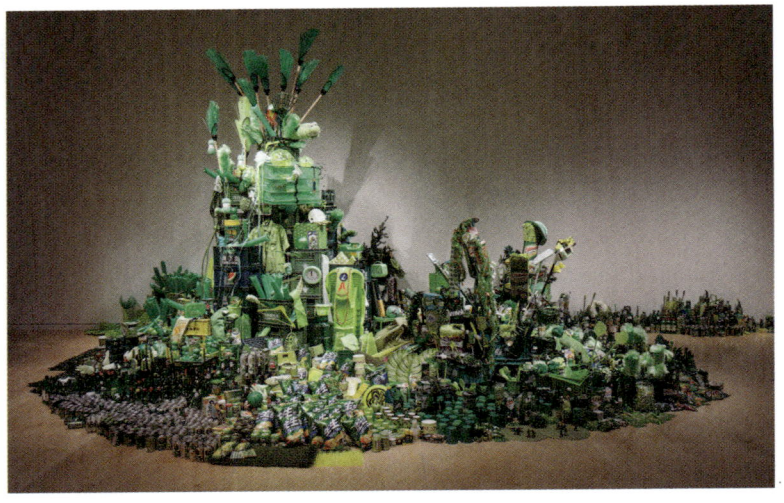

Figure 23 Han Seok Hyun, *Super-Natural*, 2011. Mixed media, mass-produced products, dimensions variable. Museum of Fine Arts, Boston. Courtesy of the artist.

with equally sharpened weaponry. His mixed-media works, such as *Super-Natural* (2011), aim to stun the viewer at first. Walking into a room, one encounters a literal landscape of hills and valleys, vistas and dramatic cliffs, made of green objects. A closer look reveals that this massive form is constituted of individual consumer products and grocery story items including children's toys, umbrellas, shelving, watering cans, brooms. The only consistency is that all the objects are green and all are easily purchasable in a store. Everyday objects, all disposable, reassembled to create an island in the middle of the gallery or museum floor. At first glance it might seem humorous and cheeky, all these silly products in their million shades of green, stacked and spread out, some seeming very steady, some very precarious. It does look like a landscape, and it does beg to be climbed on, or over, and the viewer is tossed between looking at the whole and looking at the smaller bits and parts.

Yet Han, like Hegarty, is playing a wicked visual game. For what seems whimsical, even visually delightful, quickly becomes oppressive: all the repeating patterns, all the shiny plastic, all the wastefulness in this assemblage of objects, none of them really necessary. This is after all, not a natural landscape but, as the title suggests, some steroid nightmare of consumption, plastics, and green. A color so often associated with the environment, with nature, with purity quickly moves from familiar to being too sweet, too minty, too overwhelming.

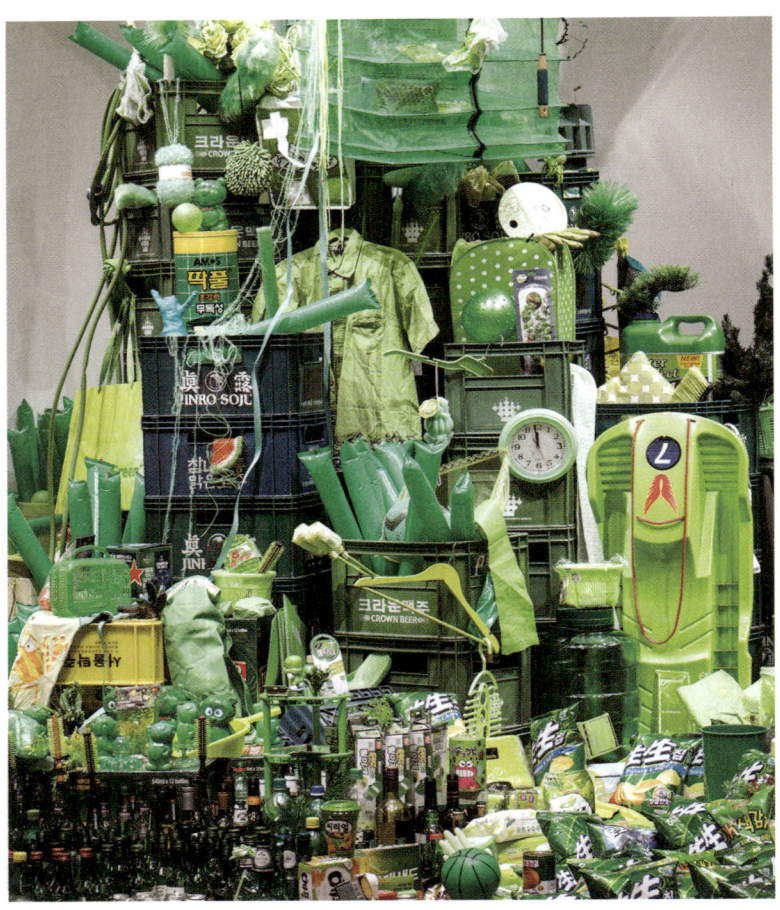

Figure 24 Han Seok Hyun, *Super-Natural*, 2011, detail. Mixed media, mass-produced products, dimensions variable. Museum of Fine Arts, Boston. Courtesy of the artist.

If many viewers' first visual association with the installation is of traditional landscapes (think here of the Korean scrolls earlier in this chapter), the more one looks at the piece the more one might see instead all the now-familiar images of plastic waste, of the floating islands of plastics that have been swirled together in the ocean. Han is directly speaking in this piece, as in much of his work, to the fate of his hometown of Seoul, but simultaneously to the larger environmental picture.[33] As the viewer is made to walk through these spaces and move from affection to repulsion, Han creates new meanings in looking at the land, and new meanings of time. When might be too late, but Han pushes the viewer to look.

***

Photographer Scott Wallace's *Eritrea* (2004) captures the ways in which we as viewers are asked to see our planet in strange and often complex ways. The poster in the image is part of a safe-sex campaign encouraging the use of condoms to confront the spread of AIDS. The message, written in three languages, is the only text on the poster. It is up to the viewer to make the necessary visual associations: a couple on a beach, a sunset, a dolphin jumping in the air. In the photograph, the landscape of this poster, which was manipulated to speak to a very specific human concern, gets dropped into another landscape. Wallace

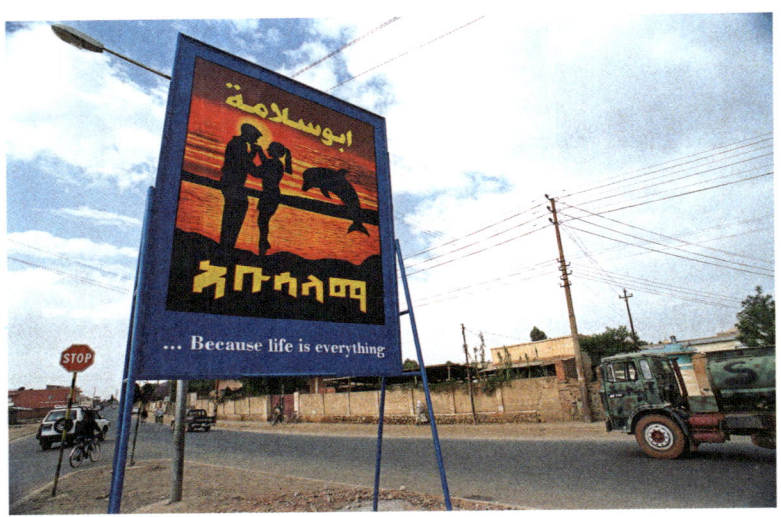

Figure 25 Scott Wallace, *Eritrea*, 2004. Photograph. Image courtesy of the artist.

neatly captures the dissonance of the image and its display in a busy intersection. It is such a unique advertising poster, but of course how many people (save Wallace) actually really look at it in this moment, in this place? Or was that the point all along, to make an image of love, sex, death, oceans, and dolphins that is viewed but maybe not deeply considered? The advertisement then just seeps into the unconscious, bumping into all our other images of love, sex, death, oceans, and dolphins. Wallace pulls it back, highlighting how we see the land, the earth, animals,

We need to know more about how our visual cultures are produced and really look at what we visually consume all day. We need to know what authorities and biases and histories are embedded in the images and things. We need to be able to accept some and reject others.

nature, in a myriad of competing ways all the time. What sticks? When will all this matter?

How the picture of the black hole was made matters. It is all right to be wary of machines, but they are not the problem. We know the problem. We need to know more about how our visual cultures are produced and really look at what we visually consume all day. We need to know what authorities and biases and histories are embedded in the images and things. We need to be able to accept some and reject others. We need to remember that Ghosh is not merely whispering in our ear; he is yelling and pleading and begging. We need to see the land. We need to see that *when* is right now.

CONCLUSION

I am less interested in the pole stars than in the
constellations, and in the dark spaces between the lights.
Caitlin Horrocks[1]

The portrait of Daniel Ward (1765–1767; Museum of the Early Southern Decorative Arts, Winston-Salem) is fairly generic as eighteenth-century portraits go, of a young wealthy white child in the American South, dressed in gorgeous silks, one hand resting on his faithful dog, the other pointing to his plantation home and the basis of his current and future income. It goes without saying that this plantation was worked by enslaved peoples, generations of whom might have gazed upon this portrait of their owner's ancestor hanging on the wall. That might have been the end of the story of the portrait; it would have lived its days, finding its way to a museum or through an auction house, or more likely being installed above a fireplace, perhaps tucked away in an attic. Yet, as art historian Jennifer Van Horn recounts, sometime during the Civil War the portrait took a detour from this mundane future.[2] The portrait of Ward was taken off the wall in the plantation house by an enslaved person, and this enslaved person then took it into their home, covered the painting with newspaper, and repurposed it to use as a fire screen.

Just like that, a portrait became something else, meant something else, and was changed. These acts of taking the painting, covering it with a newspaper (considered by whites to be a dangerous object in the hands of enslaved people for fear they could use it to pass information and to learn truths about politics and opportunities), and making it into a useful, comforting, decorative household item changed its meaning. As Van Horn astutely notes, with this transformation "enslaved people erased or overwrote the portrait's intended messages of white dominance and power."[3] What was once a symbol of violence and subjugation became a source of comfort and protection for the black body and family.

The painting, in other words, moved from being one kind of weapon to being another. Thus, even when the story takes another turn—when the white family retrieves the portrait, has it cleaned, and donates it to a museum to take its place among other markers of elite whiteness and legacy wealth—the painting cannot go back to the way it was. It had taken on new meanings and new ways of moving in the world. It had been made to represent and naturalize one kind of power structure, but now will always represent the fragility of that power and of whiteness. It signals the strength of people and of visual objects themselves to change narratives, rearrange power, to change sight.

It is so very easy to get overwhelmed by images. The visual atmosphere can often feel suffocating, with both too much and too little of substance competing for our attention. One solution to this overload is the strategy of isolation, of shutting down, of trying to eliminate the narrative. Indeed, this ideology of slowing, stopping, or interrupting the story can have obvious upsides, for if we stop trying to attach meaning and intentions to objects or representations, we might be more present. Don't interpret, in other words, just be.

But I hope this book has persuaded you that we cannot be passive to visual culture, we cannot eliminate the narratives of our visual worlds; we cannot really just be. We can let it all happen to us, but nothing will change, nothing will get better, and nothing will stick. We need to create narratives and listen critically to the stories that visual culture tells us. We definitely need to stay present, we need to fight, and we need to see the visual change and to change with it.

Indeed, notions of seeing itself are expanding with new research and theories concerning neuroaesthetics, neuro–art history, and neuroethics. These new areas of study have emerged with the increasing sophistication of brain imaging technologies. With more advanced understandings of how the brain and the eyes operate together come new questions about the visual. This is true of research in artificial intelligence as well. Brain science is going to change the visual culture game, of that there is little doubt.[4] There is so much space for all this new knowledge about how and why we see or don't see that neuroscience will demand that we ask new questions and likewise that we keep watch for new problems. Yet, in keeping with the language of Caitlin Horrocks, while neurobiology will help us with the pole stars, visual culture has always been about the constellations and the dark spaces. What "we" can see or won't see physically and biologically will need to confront how the visual shifts and changes once it hits the ground.

Practice is what is needed, habitual repetitions of thinking harder about all images and our visual atmospheres. We all need to take visual culture more seriously, we need to engage more readily, we need to be watchful and open but careful all at once. We need to think all the time about who benefits from images and how. In short, we need to constantly be thinking about the what, where, who, and when of the visual.

But make no mistake, in positing the hopeful possibilities of visual culture, I do so through the tactics of what scholar Sara Ahmed calls the "killjoy." We must not let the visual run over us. Artist Trevor Paglen warns us, "The invisible world of images isn't simply an alternative taxonomy of visuality. It is an active, cunning, exercise of power, one ideally suited to molecular police and market operations—one designed to insert its tendrils into ever-smaller slices of everyday life."[5] This is a very serious, hard, and *exhausting* battle that every one of us must

Visual culture has always been inscribed by the dominant and by domination, yet it has always also contained resistance, reversal, and subversion.

wage all the time. We can't go around visual culture; we must go through it, and to go through it is to see it for the fascist, manipulative, destructive, genocidal endeavor it *has always been*, but also for the connective, vital culture it can be.

Visual culture has always been inscribed by the dominant and by domination, yet it has always also contained resistance, reversal, and subversion. Much of the scholarly work on visual culture of the past fifty years has been uncovering and exploring those moments of resistance, making them visible in new ways so they might proliferate. This is the visual weaponized as an agent for positive, unifying change. There is, after all, so much joy, peace, happiness, connection, and collaboration in the visual atmosphere. If we reject nonconfrontational consumption of the visual, our choice can, Ahmed says, "open a life, to make room for life, to make room for possibility, for chance."[6] This is hard work, but the urgency of our historical moment demands that we all become visual activists. We must reject passivity and mere consumption, picking and choosing among preselected objects and visual theories, sidestepping that mess in the aisle to look away from disarray. Visual culture has always been the vehicle of tremendous potential and the carrier of infinite injustice. We must be more assertive, tricky, and thoughtful with our visual atmosphere. Just look around; it is totally possible.

GLOSSARY

Aesthetics
A philosophical category, but more typically used as a term to describe the logic and language of our preferences for certain objects, styles, and images. Aesthetics, in this study, is considered to be personal and cultural, not inherent, natural, or "real."

Anthropocene
A controversial geologic term which posits that human interactions with and manipulations of the planet constitute a new geological epoch. The exact timeframe for this epoch remains in dispute: some suggest it should start with the agricultural revolution while others argue for more recent start dates such as the industrial revolution or even the rise of atomic energy and weaponry. Use of the term implies that we need to take human impact on the planet (climate change, for example) far more seriously. Many scholars have significant issues with this designation and have offered alternative terminology and different strategies for confronting environmental issues, while others have rejected altogether arguments for human causality or impact that would mandate the naming of a new epoch.

Art/artist
A designation that names some visual objects and their creators as having more value as signifiers of meaning, value, beauty, creativity, and gravitas. A work of "art" is often considered precious in its singularity. Likewise, artists are granted cultural and often moral significance for what are perceived to be their innate creativity and genius. What constitutes and is valued as art shifts over time and is related to larger cultural and national power dynamics. Objects of value and their creators have been celebrated worldwide and throughout history, but the categories of "art" and "artist" are specific to certain geographies and time periods. Many today reject both terms as inherently Eurocentric, imperialist, and exclusionary.

Art history
The academic study of art, artists, and more recently broader categories of visual culture. Art history historically was deeply embedded in dialogues that

created and solidified "the canon." More recently art history as a discipline has attempted to consider visual culture in broader and more global contexts and with more self-reflection about its participation in creating categories of exclusion.

Art world

A shorthand term that encompasses a community of artists, gallery owners, museum staff, museum patrons and donors, auction house staff, visual culture critics, art historians, visual culture scholars, and general consumers/customers of art and visual culture. Some sit comfortably in this world and embrace this term as descriptive of their communities while seeking to promote and expand the definition of art and its potential. Others work actively to expand, diversify, dismantle, or mock "art world" institutions, people, and their mores for their elitism, snobbery, and misplaced sense of importance.

Canon

Objects and images that are designated as the most important works of art of an era or place, that have been singled out in art history texts, art history classrooms, museum spaces, and among those in the art world, as signifying art that is the best, the most beautiful, timeless, exclusive, and of the greatest contribution to culture. In the past fifty years, there have been significant moves to expand the canon to include work by women and people of color and more art produced outside of North America and Europe. Others have called for an end to the canon altogether, seeking to displace structural hierarchies of value.

Corporeal

As applied to visual objects, used of those that confront the nature of the body; also, of a way of thinking about the visual that actively considers physical manifestations (such as size, taste, smell, etc.) and emotional reactions (repulsion, desire, agitation, etc.) as part of the experience of sight.

Gaze

The act of looking at something; of assuming the power (or being visually guided to assume the power) of consuming what is being seen. Conversely, the experience of being consumed and subsumed by sight—of being looked at. The notion of the gaze is fundamental to the work of visual culture and film studies scholars who draw upon the psychoanalytic theories of Sigmund Freud and Jacques Lacan, among others. It is helpful to think of the gaze as a form of power and control for both the viewer and the viewed. The gaze is not pure sight, but designates the manipulated power of vision.

Kitsch

Commonly used as a negative term for an object or style considered to be in bad taste; thus, the opposite of art. The supposed political and social malevolence of kitsch was most forcefully articulated by twentieth-century critic Clement Greenberg, who posited kitsch as the enemy of art because it was manufactured for, and catered to, the basic desires of the general public and encouraged cheap sentimentality. Art, on the other hand, pushed society and people forward toward progressive and enlightened states, Greenberg argued; it made humanity better. The term "kitsch" is also typically used to disparage the low- and middlebrow tastes of the unsophisticated masses, fueling accusations of elitism in the art world. Notably, Greenberg frames art and music produced outside of a European or North American context as "folk" and therefore peripheral to both oppositional categories, kitsch and art.

Landscape

A constructed visualization of land, sky, or ocean. A landscape can never be a natural or true representation of a place since it depends on choices and decisions: the maker captures a particular scene in a specific moment by highlighting certain visual elements or qualities. Landscapes are often used as visual manifestations of wealth, nationalism, political ideology, and/or spirituality.

Low/high culture

Used individually or together, these terms delineate the status distinctions that mark and categorize all forms of visual production. Most scholars view these terms as problematic because they do not engage the intersectional complications of access, pleasure, or the structural inequalities of race, gender, sexuality, ability, etc. In the twentieth century, makers and audiences began to play with and intentionally confuse the meanings of these categories in order to challenge their authority to define art or people.

Original/copy

Important concepts in establishing the differences between art and non-art, or kitsch. The notion of the **original** is very important to the definition of art as the product of rare skill and the manner of the creator/artist, as precious because of its singularity, and as containing what Walter Benjamin called a certain "aura" or unique quality. These characteristics make originals worth protecting (as in museums which conserve them), and validate their often-extraordinary monetary value. **Copies** are by definition not unique. In visual culture, they may be prints, photographs, digital traces, 3D print replications, etc. Some copies can be almost as valuable as their original if they are limited in quantity (the numbered print, for example) or have been manipulated in some way. But generally a copy is deemed less important, less creative, and of much less worth than an original. In the twentieth century and still today, the relationship between a copy and an original became one of the most generative and provocative concepts in visual culture and artistic production. Numerous makers have played with the idea of copies and disposability as potentially more valuable than honoring an original.

Self-portrait/selfie

A **self-portrait** is the visual depiction of oneself made by oneself. A traditional subject for fine artists, self-portraits are typically considered most interesting and important if they not only represent the physicality of a person but some specific aspect of their personality or a quality of emotion. A **selfie** can be considered a self-portrait that has been made and then proliferated using the technologies of the digital camera, the cell phone, and the platforms of Instagram and Facebook. Traditional self-portraits needed museums, galleries, public buildings, and homes for display and thus were somewhat limited in terms of visual saturation, while the creation of a self-portrait demanded a particular set of materials and skills. The cell phone, however, has made the self-portrait vastly easier both to produce and to circulate. In contemporary society, the selfie is often negatively associated with femininity and vanity, but this may be a way to diminish the positive self-expressive potential of new technology and the greater ability it gives individuals to produce their own visual culture.

Visual atmosphere

The constellation of objects, images, impulses, and tones that create a visual space and moment. To understand a scene, place, or specific moment in time, we cannot focus on the isolated impacts of individual objects and images. Instead, we must be attentive to how the objects react with each other, the histories and memories that are being evoked, and the plays of tone and their manipulations. A visual atmosphere is totalizing, like the air we breathe. It is everywhere and might go unnoticed or be taken for granted; or it can obscure, disorient, and even suffocate.

Visuality
Beyond the biological function of looking, visuality describes the process of computing the broader social and cultural context and constructions of sight and its impacts. The eye inputs data, which must be sorted—this sorting is the crux of visuality. More recently, visual culture scholar Nicholas Mirzoeff has rearticulated the impact of visuality as a conceptual frame, one we can productively think against or reclaim in new ways.

NOTES

Introduction
1. Michel-Rolph Trouillot, *Silencing the Past: Power and the Production of History* (Boston: Beacon Press, 1995), xxiii.
2. Umbro Apollonio, ed., *Documents of 20th Century Art: Futurist Manifestos*, translated by Robert Brain, R. W. Flint, J. C. Higgitt, and Caroline Tisdall (New York: Viking Press, 1973), 19–24.
3. Allan deSouza, *How Art Can Be Thought: A Handbook for Change* (Durham: Duke University Press, 2018), 13.

Chapter 1
1. For a helpful summary of this work in the context of the global movement of objects, see Marita Sturken and Lisa Cartwright, *Practices of Looking: An Introduction to Visual Culture*, 3rd ed. (New York: Oxford University Press, 2018), 390.
2. See https://rhizome.org/download/#works, accessed January 26, 2020.
3. See https://additivism.org/about, accessed August 11, 2019.
4. Morehshin Allahyari and Daniel Rourke, "The 3D Additivist Manifesto," in *The 3D Additivist Cookbook*, edited by Morehshin Allahyari and Daniel Rourke (Amsterdam: Institute of Network Cultures, 2016), https://www.scribd.com/document/333134915/The-3D-Additivist-Cookbook#, accessed August 11, 2019.
5. Alexis Anais Avedisian and Anna Khachiyan, "On Material Speculation," essay for exhibition, Trinity Square Video, Toronto, 2016; see http://www.morehshin.com/wp-content/uploads/2016/03/morehshin_allahyari-material_speculation_isis_brochure-1.pdf, accessed August 10, 2019.
6. For more on the myth and its popularity and interpretations, see Abbie Garrington, *Excursus: Pygmalion* (Edinburgh: Edinburgh University Press, 2013), 52–72; Kathy McConnell, *Pain, Porn and Complicity: Women Heroes from Pygmalion to Twilight* (Hamilton, ON: Wolsak and Wynn, 2012); and Kelly Dennis, *Art/Porn: A History of Seeing and Touching* (Oxford: Berg, 2009).
7. For a fantastic study of the visual imagery of graphics see Johanna Drucker, *Graphesis: Visual Forms of Knowledge Production* (Cambridge, MA: Harvard University Press, 2014). Equally smart is Manuel Lima, *Visual Complexity: Mapping Patterns of Information* (New York: Princeton Architectural Press, 2011).

8. Lauren Cornell and Ed Halter, eds., *Mass Effect: Art and the Internet in the Twenty-First Century* (Cambridge, MA: MIT Press and New Museum, 2015), 105.

9. See Joanna Zylinska, *Nonhuman Photography* (Cambridge, MA: MIT Press, 2017).

10. Saidiya Hartman, *Scenes of Subjection: Terror, Slavery, and Self-Making in Nineteenth Century America* (New York: Oxford University Press, 1997), 3.

11. See too Nicholas Mirzoeff, *The Right to Look: A Counterhistory of Visuality* (Durham: Duke University Press, 2011).

12. Scott Wallace, "Why Revealing Uncontacted Tribes May Help Save Them," *National Geographic*, November 21, 2018, https://www.nationalgeographic.com/culture/2018/08/brazil-uncontacted-tribe-indigenous-people-amazon-video/, accessed August 11, 2019.

13. https://www.youtube.com/watch?time_continue=87&v=kvfJBijV4XQ, accessed July 28, 2019.

14. Wallace, "Why Revealing Uncontacted Tribes May Help Save Them."

15. A. C. Thompson, "Inside the Secret Border Patrol Facebook Group Where Agents Joke about Migrant Deaths and Post Sexist Memes," *ProPublica*, July 1, 2019, https://www.propublica.org/article/secret-border-patrol-facebook-group-agents-joke-about-migrant-deaths-post-sexist-memes?fbclid=IwAR04J85h0KI9MCOyyXeyNtue3-4kW0F_g94adoqUAoIJgK36rQzcrj2zAlM, accessed August 11, 2019.

16. Kevin Moxey gives one of the most concise summaries of this disciplinary and ideological history of thinking about images in his *Visual Time: The Image in History* (Durham: Duke University Press, 2013), 53–75.

17. Donna Haraway, *Simians, Cyborgs, and Women: The Reinvention of Natures* (New York: Routledge, 1991), 151.

18. For a few versions of the visual culture origin story see Margaret Dikovitskaya, *Visual Culture: The Study of the Visual after the Cultural Turn* (Cambridge, MA: MIT Press, 2005), 6–45; Aruna D'Souza, "Introduction," in *Art History in the Wake of the Global Turn*, edited by Jill H. Casid and Aruna D'Souza (Williamstown, MA: Clark Art Institute, 2014), x; Nicholas Mirzoeff, *How to See the World* (London: Penguin, 2015), 12; Sturken and Cartwright, *Practices of Looking*, 7–8.

19. A succinct summary can be found by Neil Mulholland, "Definitions of Art and the Art World," in *Exploring Visual Culture: Definitions, Concepts, Contexts*, edited by Matthew Rampley (Edinburgh: Edinburgh University Press, 2005), 18–33. Also helpful is Whitney Davis, *A General Theory of Visual Culture* (Princeton: Princeton University Press, 2018).

20. To name just a few of the transformative art historical writers, think Heinrich Wölfflin, Meyer Schapiro, Erwin Panofsky, and Ernst Gombrich.

21. Benjamin remains one of the most important and influential theorists of the visual. His essay "The Work of Art in the Age of Mechanical Reproduction," written in 1936, is still required reading for those interested in the visual. His monumental and unfinished *Arcades Project* (1927–1940) similarly is rich with potential about seeing, even in this contemporary moment.

22. Kevin Moxey, "Motivating History," *Art Bulletin* 77, no. 3 (September 1995): 392.

23. Sturkin and Cartwright, *Practices of Looking*, 5.

24. In thinking about perception as a historically constructed category, see Jonathan Crary, *Suspensions of Perception: Attention, Spectacle, and Modern Culture* (Cambridge, MA: MIT Press, 1999). See too Anne Friedberg, *Window Shopping: Cinema and the Postmodern* (Berkeley: University of California Press, 1994), and Martin Jay, *Downcast Eyes: The Denigration of Vision in Twentieth-Century French Thought* (Berkeley: University of California Press, 1993).

25. Mirzoeff, *How to See the World*, 11.

26. Sturkin and Cartwright, *Practices of Looking*, 7

27. For more on these meanings and definitions, see *What Is an Image?*, edited by James Elkins and Maja Naef (University Park: Penn State University Press, 2011).

28. Kandice Chuh, *The Difference Aesthetics Makes* (Durham: Duke University Press, 2019), 5.

29. The video was first shown at a concert on June 16, 2018. It is six minutes long and was directed by Ricky Saiz: https://vimeo.com/294517212, accessed July 30, 2019.

30. See for example Rikki Byrd, "Beyoncé and Jay-Z's 'Apeshit' Video Shows Black Bodies in Art—and in Control," *Racked*, June 18, 2018, https://www.racked.com/2018/6/18/17476770/beyonce-jay-z-apeshit-everything-is-love-art-meaning-louvre; Taylor Hosking, "Beyoncé and Jay-Z's New Vision of Gender in 'Apeshit'," *Atlantic*, June 22, 2018, https://www.theatlantic.com/entertainment/archive/2018/06/beyonce-and-jay-zs-new-way-of-looking-at-gender/563360/; Cady Lang, "Art History Experts Explain the Meaning of the Art in Beyoncé and Jay-Z's 'Apesh-t' Video," *Time*, June 19, 2018, https://time.com/5315275/art-references-meaning-beyonce-jay-z-apeshit-louvre-music-video/; Doreen St. Félix, "The Power and Paradox of Beyoncé and Jay-Z Taking Over the Louvre," *New Yorker*, June 19, 2018, https://www.newyorker.com/culture/culture-desk/what-it-means-when-beyonce-and-jay-z-take-over-the-louvre; all accessed November 4, 2019.

31. See for example Amy E. Herman, *Visual Intelligence: Sharpen Your Perception, Change Your Life* (New York: Houghton Mifflin Harcourt, 2016); James Elkins, *How to Use Your Eyes* (New York: Routledge, 2000); and Alain de Botton, *Art as Therapy* (London: Phaidon, 2013).

32. Nicholas Mirzoeff, "Ghostwriting: Working Out Visual Culture," in *Art History, Aesthetics, Visual Studies*, edited by Michael Ann Holly and Keith Moxey (Williamstown, MA: Clark Art Institute, 2002), 190.

33. Hito Steyerl, "In Defense of the Poor Image," *e-flux journal* #10 (November 2009), https://www.e-flux.com/journal/10/61362/in-defense-of-the-poor-image/, accessed August 11, 2019.

Chapter 2

1. Akiko Busch, *How to Disappear: Notes on Invisibility in a Time of Transparency* (New York: Penguin Press, 2019), 3.

2. The notice is no longer available on the Walker Art Center webpage, although this is the dead link: https://walkerart.org/magazine/cultivating-the-garden-for-art-curatorial-and-civic-thinking-behind-a-reanimated-green-space?_ga=2.63650662.857527365.1564526816-44935773.1564526816. The notice is mentioned in Olga Viso's first apology statement released the following day, "Learning in Public: An Open Letter on Sam Durant's Scaffold," May 26, 2017, https://walkerart.org/magazine/learning-in-public-an-open-letter-on-sam-durants-scaffold, accessed July 30, 2019.

3. A description of the work from Sam Durant's webpage; now removed. See http://web.archive.org/web/20161017112101/http://www.samdurant.net:80/index.php?/projects/scaffold/, accessed August 2, 2019.

4. Viso, "Learning in Public."

5. From Durant's removed text from his website, http://web.archive.org/web/20161017112101/http://www.samdurant.net:80/index.php?/projects/scaffold/

6. Viso, "Learning in Public."

7. Sheila Regan, "After Protest from Native American Community, Walker Art Center Will Remove Public Sculpture," *Hyperallergic*, May 29, 2017, https://hyperallergic.com/382141/after-protests-from-native-american-community-walker-art-center-will-remove-public-sculpture/, accessed August 2, 2019.

8. "A Statement from Olga Viso," posted on the Walker Center's Facebook page, May 27, 2017, https://www.facebook.com/walkerartcenter/posts/10155306124008180, accessed August 2, 2019.

9. Andy Battaglia, Sarah Douglas, and Andrew Russeth, "After Announcement That Olga Viso Will Step Down as Walker Director, Museum Professionals

Largely Praise Handling of 'Scaffold' Controversy," *ArtNews*, November 17, 2017, http://www.artnews.com/2017/11/17/announcement-olga-viso-will-step-walker-director-museum-professionals-largely-praise-handling-scaffold-controversy/, accessed August 2, 2019.

10. Ashley Fairbanks, "Genocide and Mini-golf in the Walker Sculpture Garden," *Citypages*, May 27, 2017, http://www.citypages.com/arts/genocide-and-mini-golf-in-the-walker-sculpture-garden/424797173, accessed August 2, 2019.

11. For a summary of the history of the work and its reception see Jane F. Gerhard, *The Dinner Party: Judy Chicago and the Power of Popular Feminism, 1970–2007* (Athens: University of Georgia Press, 2013) esp. 211–282.

12. Elizabeth A. Sackler is related to the Sacklers involved in the opiate/pharmaceutical lawsuits, which also impacted the art world as the Sackler family donated to many arts institutions. Her branch of the family, however, had divested from the company involved in the lawsuits before its promotion of opiates began.

13. Michael Kelly, "Danto and Krauss on Cindy Sherman," in *Art History, Aesthetics, Visual Studies*, edited by Michael Ann Holly and Keith Moxey (Williamstown, MA: Clark Art Institute, 2002), 128.

14. Helpful in thinking about the issues of the impact of colonialism on museums is *Art History in the Wake of the Global Turn*, edited by Jill H. Casid and Aruna D'Souza (Williamstown, MA: Clark Art Institute, 2014).

15. Emily L. Moore, *Proud Raven, Panting Wolf* (Seattle: University of Washington Press, 2018), 6–7.

16. For classic sources on the history of museums and the history of collecting, see: Tony Bennett, *The Birth of the Museum* (London: Routledge, 1995); David Carrier, *Museum Skepticism: A History of the Display of Art in Public Galleries* (Durham: Duke University Press, 2006); Douglas Crimp, *On the Museum's Ruins* (Cambridge, MA: MIT Press, 1993); and Carol Duncan, *Civilizing Rituals: Inside Public Art Museums* (London: Routledge, 1995).

17. Svetlana Alpers, "The Museum as a Way of Seeing," in *Exhibiting Cultures: The Poetics and Politics of Museum Display*, edited by Ivan Karp and Steven D. Lavine (Washington, DC: Smithsonian Institution Press, 1991), 27.

18. David Carrier and Joachim Pissarro, *Aesthetic of the Margins/The Margins of Aesthetics* (University Park: Penn State University Press, 2019), 191.

19. Bennett, *The Birth of the Museum*, 126.

20. For a great study of African art and French museum history see Sally Price, *Paris Primitive: Jacques Chirac's Museum on the Quai Branly* (Chicago: University of Chicago Press, 2007).

21. Moore, *Proud Raven, Panting Wolf*, 4.

22. See Haidy Geismar, *Museum Object Lessons for the Digital Age* (London: UCL Press, 2018).

23. For a full analysis of Kinkade and dialogues about visual culture see *Thomas Kinkade: The Artist in the Mall*, edited by Alexis L. Boylan (Durham: Duke University Press, 2011).

24. Clement Greenberg, "Avant-Garde and Kitsch," in *Clement Greenberg: The Collected Essays and Criticism*, edited by John O'Brian, vol. 1 (Chicago: University of Chicago Press, 1986), 5–22.

25. For a smart essay on this period of seeing and not seeing coffins in relation to military policy see Rebecca A. Adelman, "The 'Coffin,' the Camera, and the Commodity: Visualizing American Military Dead at Dover," in *On Not Looking: The Paradox of Contemporary Visual Culture*, edited by Frances Guerin (New York: Routledge, 2015), 229–250.

26. Marlon Bailey, *Butch Queens Up in Pumps: Gender, Performance, and Ballroom Culture in Detroit* (Ann Arbor: University of Michigan Press, 2013), 4.

27. Much has been written about Livingston's film, as well as Madonna's videos. While they are a bit dated, still crucial reading on these productions are bell hooks, *Black Looks: Race and Representation* (Boston: South End Press, 1992), 145–156, and Judith Butler, *Bodies That Matter* (London: Routledge, 1993), 121–140.

28. Allan deSouza, *How Art Can Be Thought: A Handbook for Change* (Durham: Duke University Press, 2018), 13.

29. Gregory Sholette, *Delirium and Resistance: Activist Art and the Crisis of Capitalism*, edited by Kim Charnley (London: Pluto Press, 2017), 52.

Chapter 3

1. Bruce Springsteen, "Pink Cadillac," released in 1984 as the B-side of "Dancing in the Dark."

2. Mike Allen, "Obama Slams New Yorker Portrayal," *Politico*, July 13, 2008, https://www.politico.com/story/2008/07/obama-slams-new-yorker-portrayal-011719, accessed August 14, 2019.

3. Nico Pitney, "Barry Blitt Defends His New Yorker Cover of Obama," *HuffPost*, July 21, 2008, https://www.huffpost.com/entry/barry-blitt-addresses-his_n_112432, accessed August 14, 2019.

4. Rachel Sklar, "David Remnick on That New Yorker Cover: It's Satire, Meant to Target 'Distortions and Misconceptions and Prejudices' about Obama," *HuffPost*, July 21, 2008, https://www.huffpost.com/entry/david-remnick-on-emnew-yo_n_112456, accessed August 29, 2019.

5. Feminist interventions are crucial here, and film theorist Laura Mulvey's work is an oft-cited voice. Likewise, the work of art historian Griselda Pollock, and that of Tania Modleski in regard to this gaze in television and film, are fundamental. The intersectional ramifications for the gaze will be discussed later in this chapter.

6. Nicholas Mirzoeff, *The Right to Look: A Counterhistory of Visuality* (Durham: Duke University Press, 2011), 1.

7. See *On Not Looking: The Paradox of Contemporary Visual Culture*, edited by Frances Guerin (New York: Routledge, 2015), and *Unwatchable*, edited by Nicholas Baer, Maggie Hennefeld, Laura Horak, and Gunnar Iversen (New Brunswick, NJ: Rutgers University Press, 2019).

8. For a brief history of the term see Derek Conrad Murray, "Notes to Self: The Visual Culture of Selfies in the Age of Social Media," *Consumption Markets and Culture* 18, no. 6 (2015): 491–492. See too Nicholas Mirzoeff, *How to See the World* (London: Penguin, 2015), 31–33 and 62–69.

9. Celia Walden, "We Take 1 Million Selfies Every Day—but What Are They Doing to Our Brains?," *Telegraph*, May 24, 2016, https://www.telegraph.co.uk/women/life/we-take-1-million-selfies-every-day---but-what-are-they-doing-to/, accessed August 16, 2019; and Sarah Cascone, "24 Billion Photos Prove Our Selfie Obsession Is Out of Control," *Art News*, June 1, 2016, https://news.artnet.com/art-world/24-billion-selfies-uploaded-to-google-in-a-year-508718, accessed August 29, 2019.

10. For a nuanced discussion of both these positions, see *Selfie Nation*, edited by Adi Kuntsman (London: Palgrave Macmillan, 2017).

11. Derek Conrad Murray, "Selfie Consumerism in a Narcissistic Age," *Consumption Markets and Culture* 23, no. 1 (2020): 21–43.

12. Martin Graff, "Are You Taking Too Many Selfies?," *Psychology Today*, April 26, 2018, https://www.psychologytoday.com/us/blog/love-digitally/201804/are-you-taking-too-many-selfies; and "Too Many Selfies?," *CBS News*, February 21, 2018, https://www.cbsnews.com/news/too-many-selfies-you-may-have-selfitis/, accessed August 29, 2019.

13. Sara Tasker, *Hashtag Authentic* (London: White Lion Publishing, 2019), 13.

14. John Berger, *Ways of Seeing* (London: BBC and Penguin Books, 1972), 46–47.

15. Ruth Curry, "Toward a Unified Theory of Kim Kardashian," *Brooklyn Magazine*, September 14, 2014, http://www.bkmag.com/2014/09/10/toward-a-unified-theory-of-kim-kardashian-hollywood/, accessed August 16, 2019. See

too Murray, "Selfie Consumerism in a Narcissistic Age," for a reading of the feminist potential of selfies.

16. Hillary Clinton, DNC Women's Leadership Forum, Marriott Marquis Hotel, Washington, DC, September 19, 2014, http://www.p2016.org/clinton/clinton091914spt.html, accessed August 17, 2019.

17. Arielle Azoulay, *The Civil Contract of Photography* (Cambridge, MA: MIT Press, 2008), 269.

18. See https://projectunbreakable.tumblr.com/post/18913383586/faq, accessed August 17, 2019.

19. Anemona Hartocollis, "Taking on Harvard over Rights to Slave Photos," *New York Times*, March 21, 2019, Section A, 1.

20. See Aruna D'Souza's sharp and insightful *Whitewalling: Art, Race, and Protest in 3 Acts* (New York: Badlands Unlimited, 2018) for a longer treatment of the visual consequences of the Whitney's handling of this incident and the more profound history of African American conflict with white-controlled museum spaces.

21. Tom Gunning, "Truthiness and the More Real: What Is the Difference?," in Elizabeth Armstrong et al., *More Real? Art in the Age of Truthiness* (Minneapolis: Minneapolis Institute of Arts; Munich: Delmonico Books/Prestel, 2012), 179.

22. Sarah Lewis, "The Racial Bias Built into Photography," *New York Times*, April 25, 2019, https://www.nytimes.com/2019/04/25/lens/sarah-lewis-racial-bias-photography.html#, accessed April 17, 2019.

23. Clemens Apprich, "Introduction," in Clemens Apprich, Wendy Hui Kyong Chun, Florian Cramer, and Hito Steyerl, *Pattern Discrimination* (Minneapolis: University of Minnesota Press, 2019), x.

24. Michael Omi and Howard Winant answer this question more directly, arguing that "there is a crucial and non-reducible visual dimension to the definition and understanding of racial categories." See Omi and Winant, *Racial Formation in the United States* (New York: Routledge, 2015), 111. Thanks to the outside reviewer for this note and for pushing this question.

25. Johanna Burton, "Irreconcilable Difference," in *Trigger: Gender as a Tool and a Weapon*, edited by Johanna Burton and Natalie Bell (New York: New Museum, 2017), 15.

26. Mirzoeff, *The Right to Look*, 1 and 309.

27. For an article on the intersectional potential of Thomas's work see Derek Conrad Murray, "Afro-Kitsch and the Queering of Blackness," *American Art* 28, no. 1 (Spring 2014): 9–15.

28. Huey Copeland and Krista Thompson, "Afrotropes: A User's Guide," *Art Journal* 76 (Fall-Winter 2017): 7.

29. Hito Steyerl, *The Wretched of the Screen* (Berlin: Sternberg Press, 2012), 187.

30. See Lyra D. Monteiro, "Race-Conscious Casting and the Erasure of the Black Past in Lin-Manuel Miranda's Hamilton," *Public Historian* 38, no. 1 (February 2016): 89–98.

31. For more on contemporary visual dialogues about migration see T. J. Demos, *The Migrant Image: The Art and Politics of Documentary during Global Crisis* (Durham: Duke University Press, 2013).

32. Kobena Mercer, "Photography's Time of Dispersal and Return," in *Art History in the Wake of the Global Turn*, edited by Jill H. Casid and Aruna D'Souza (Williamstown, MA: Clark Art Institute, 2014), 71.

33. Steyerl, *The Wretched of the Screen*, 168.

Chapter 4

1. Press release, "Astronomers Capture First Picture of Black Hole," https://eventhorizontelescope.org/, accessed August 24, 2019.

2. Nicholas Mirzoeff, *How to See the World* (London: Penguin, 2015), 4.

3. For a smart analysis of images of the moon, particularly in regard to the advent of photography, see Mia Fineman and Beth Saunders, *Apollo's Muse: The Moon in the Age of Photography* (New York: Metropolitan Museum of Art; New Haven: Yale University Press, 2019).

4. Ota Lutz, "How Scientists Captured the First Image of a Black Hole," April 19, 2019, for NASA Jet Propulsion Laboratory, California Institute of Technology, https://www.jpl.nasa.gov/edu/news/2019/4/19/how-scientists-captured-the-first-image-of-a-black-hole/, accessed August 19, 2019.

5. Ibid.

6. "Key Science Objective," from the Event Horizon Telescope website, https://eventhorizontelescope.org/science, accessed August 19, 2019.

7. Lisa Messeri, *Placing Outer Space: An Earthly Ethnography of Other Worlds* (Durham: Duke University Press, 2016), 61–62. See too the very smart study by Elizabeth A. Kessler, *Picturing the Cosmos: Hubble Space Telescope Images and the Astronomical Sublime* (Minneapolis: University of Minnesota Press, 2012).

8. Thanks to Nathan Braccio for talking me through Indigenous mapmaking. See his forthcoming dissertation, "Parallel Landscapes: Algonquian and English Spatial Understandings of New England, 1500–1700."

9. For a thoughtful critical engagement with the complexity of the visual culture of taxidermy see Rachel Poliquin, *The Breathless Zoo: Taxidermy and the Cultures of Longing* (University Park: Penn State University Press), 2012.

10. Amitav Ghosh, *The Great Derangement: Climate Change and the Unthinkable* (Chicago: University of Chicago Press, 2016), 135.

11. This is a reference to Al Gore's film *An Inconvenient Truth*. As scholar Julie Doyle notes, the polar bear has made it hard to see climate change as "a human concern in the present." See Julie Doyle, "Imaginative Engagements: Critical Reflections on Visual Arts and Climate Change," in *Art, Theory and Practice in the Anthropocene*, edited by Julie Reiss (Wilmington, DE: Vernon Press, 2019), 47.

12. See Rob Nixon, *Slow Violence and the Environmentalism of the Poor* (Cambridge, MA: Harvard University Press, 2011), 1–45.

13. Other versions of time and place and change have included arguments for seeing *the when* as the Great Acceleration, Capitalocence, Chthulucene, Homogenocene, Meghalayan. Although she is advancing her own term (Chthulucene), Haraway's explanation of the importance of these terms is helpful. See Donna Haraway, *Staying with the Trouble: Making Kin in the Chthulucene* (Durham: Duke University Press, 2016), 30–57.

14. Nicholas Mirzoeff, "Visualizing the Anthropocene," *Public Culture* 26, no. 2 (May 1, 2014): 213.

15. Donna Haraway, "Situated Knowledges: The Science Question in Feminism and the Privilege of Partial Perspective," *Feminist Studies* 14, no. 3 (Autumn 1988): 581.

16. Haraway, *Staying with the Trouble*, 1.

17. https://www.theagoraphobictraveller.com/about-the-agoraphobic-traveller.

18. Andrea DenHoed, "An Agoraphobic Photographer's Virtual Travels, on Google Street View," *New Yorker*, June 29, 2017, https://www.newyorker.com/culture/photo-booth/an-agoraphobic-photographers-virtual-travels-on-google-street-view, accessed August 19, 2019.

19. Messeri, *Placing Outer Space*, 11.

20. Ibid., 12.

21. For more on these scrolls, see https://www.metmuseum.org/toah/works-of-art/1987.278a,b/, accessed November 4, 2019.

22. T. J. Demos, *Against the Anthropocene: Visual Culture and Environment Today* (Berlin: Sternberg Press, 2017), 18.

23. Greg Milner, *Pinpoint: How GPS Is Changing Technology, Culture, and Our Minds* (New York: W. W. Norton, 2017), 269.

24. Wendy Hui Kyong Chun, *Control and Freedom: Power and Paranoia in the Age of Fiber Optics* (Cambridge, MA: MIT Press, 2006), 30.

25. Janet Vertesi, *Seeing Like a Rover: How Robots, Teams, and Images Craft Knowledge of Mars* (Chicago: University of Chicago Press, 2015), 16. See too, for insightful critique of the science of seeing, Marita Sturken and Lisa Cartwright, *Practices of Looking: An Introduction to Visual Culture*, 3rd ed. (New York: Oxford University Press, 2018), 337–378.

26. Joanna Zylinska, *Nonhuman Photography* (Cambridge, MA: MIT Press, 2017), 2.

27. Ibid., 15.

28. Alex Bush, "Breakaway," in *Unwatchable*, edited by Nicholas Baer, Maggie Hennefeld, Laura Horak, and Gunnar Iversen (New Brunswick, NJ: Rutgers University Press, 2019), 69 and 71.

29. E. Ann Kaplan, *Climate Trauma: Seeing the Future in Dystopian Film and Fiction* (New Brunswick, NJ: Rutgers University Press, 2016), 8.

30. See Alexis L. Boylan, Anna Mae Duane, Mike Gill, and Barbara Gurr, *Furious Feminisms: Alternate Routes on "Mad Max: Fury Road"* (Minneapolis: University of Minnesota Press, 2020).

31. Nixon, *Slow Violence*, 3.

32. Valerie Hegarty, email to the author, August 29, 2019.

33. For a brilliant exhibition catalogue and dialogue about Han in the context of contemporary Asian art, see Al Miner and Laura Weinstein, *Megacities Asia* (Boston: Museum of Fine Arts, 2016), esp. 105–109.

Conclusion

1. Caitlin Horrocks, "The Ordinary Woman Theory," *Paris Review*, July 30, 2019, https://www.theparisreview.org/blog/2019/07/30/the-ordinary-woman-theory/.

2. Jennifer Van Horn, "'The Dark Iconoclast': African Americans' Artistic Resistance in the Civil War South," *Art Bulletin* 99, no. 4 (2017): 133–167.

3. Ibid., 143.

4. See Anjan Chatterjee, *The Aesthetic Brain: How We Evolved to Desire Beauty and Enjoy Art* (Oxford: Oxford University Press, 2013); Eric Kandel, *Reductionism in Art and Brain Science: Bridging the Two Cultures* (New York: Columbia University Press, 2013); John Onians, *Neuroarthistory: From Aristotle and Pliny to Baxandall and Zeki* (New Haven: Yale University Press, 2007); G. Gabrielle Starr, *Feeling Beauty: The Neuroscience of Aesthetic Experience* (Cambridge, MA: MIT Press, 2013); Marine Vernet, "How Art and Neuroscience Fell for Each Other," in *Aesthetics and Neuroscience*, edited by Zoï Kapoula and Marine Vernet (Cham, Switzerland: Springer, 2016), 81–89; and Semir Zeki, *Inner*

Vision: An Exploration of Art and the Brain (Oxford: Oxford University Press, 1999). In regard to artificial intelligence, very helpful is Susan Schneider, *Artificial You: AI and the Future of your Mind* (Princeton: Princeton University Press, 2019). Finally, for a truly provocative consideration of sight, truth, and evolution see Donald Hoffman, *The Case against Reality: Why Evolution Hid the Truth from Our Eyes* (New York: W. W. Norton, 2019).

5. Trevor Paglen, "Invisible Images (Your Pictures Are Looking at You)," *New Inquiry*, December 8, 2016, https://thenewinquiry.com/invisible-images-your-pictures-are-looking-at-you/, accessed August 26, 2019. Thanks to Brian Bishop for suggesting this essay.

6. Sara Ahmed, *The Promise of Happiness* (Durham: Duke University Press, 2010), 20.

FURTHER READING

Abel, Elizabeth. *Sign of the Times: The Visual Politics of Jim Crow*. Berkeley: University of California Press, 2010.

Alsultany, Evelyn. *Arabs and Muslims in the Media: Race and Representation after 9/11*. New York: New York University Press, 2012.

Baudrillard, Jean. *The Conspiracy of Art: Manifestos, Interviews, Essays*. Cambridge, MA: Semiotext(e), 2005.

Baudrillard, Jean. *Simulacra and Simulation*. Ann Arbor: University of Michigan Press, 1994.

Berger, Martin. *Sight Unseen: Whiteness in American Visual Culture*. Berkeley: University of California Press, 2005.

Brown, Elspeth H. *The Corporate Eye: Photography and the Rationalization of American Commercial Culture, 1884–1929*. Baltimore: Johns Hopkins University Press, 2005.

Brown, Elspeth H., and Thy Phu, eds. *Feeling Photography*. Durham: Duke University Press, 2014.

Brown, Jayna. *Babylon Girls: Black Women Performers and the Shaping of the Modern*. Durham: Duke University Press, 2008.

Buszek, Maria Elena. *Pin-up Grrrls: Feminism, Sexuality, Popular Culture*. Durham: Duke University Press, 2006.

Butler, Judith. *Bodies that Matter*. London: Routledge, 1993.

Butler, Judith. *Gender Trouble*. 1996; London: Routledge, 2006.

Cartwright, Lisa. *Screening the Body: Tracing Medicine's Visual Culture*. Minneapolis: University of Minnesota Press, 1995.

Cheng, Anne Anlin. *Ornamentalism*. New York: Oxford University Press, 2019.

Cheng, Anne Anlin. *Second Skin: Josephine Baker and the Modern Surface*. Oxford: Oxford University Press, 2011.

Chun, Wendy Hui-Kyong. *Updating to Remain the Same: Habitual New Media*. Cambridge, MA: MIT Press, 2016.

Chute, Hilary. *Graphic Women: Life Narrative and Contemporary Comics*. New York: Columbia University Press, 2010.

Cornell, Lauren, and Ed Halter, eds. *Mass Effect: Art and the Internet in the Twenty-First Century*. Cambridge, MA: MIT Press; New York: New Museum, 2015.

Crimp, Douglas. *On the Museum's Ruins*. Cambridge, MA: MIT Press, 1993.

Dibazar, P., and J. A. Naeff. *Visualizing the Street: New Practices of Documenting, Navigating and Imagining the City*. Amsterdam: Amsterdam University Press, 2018.

Drucker, Johanna. *Graphesis: Visual Forms of Knowledge Production*. Cambridge, MA: Harvard University Press, 2014.

Finkelstein, Avram. *After Silence: A History of AIDS through Its Images*. Berkeley: University of California Press, 2018.

Friedberg, Anne. *Window Shopping: Cinema and the Postmodern*. Berkeley: University of California Press, 1994.

Hartman, Saidiya. *Wayward Lives, Beautiful Experiments: Intimate Histories of Social Upheaval*. New York: W. W. Norton, 2019.

hooks, bell. *Art on My Mind: Visual Politics*. New York: New Press, 1995.

Jay, Martin. *Downcast Eyes: The Denigration of Vision in Twentieth-Century French Thought*. Berkeley: University of California Press, 1993.

Jones, Amelia. *Seeing Differently: A History and Theory of Identification and the Visual Arts*. London: Routledge, 2012.

Jones, Caroline. *The Global Work of Art: World's Fairs, Biennials, and the Aesthetics of Experience*. Cambridge, MA: MIT Press, 2017.

Kina, Laura, and Jan Christian Bernabe, eds. *Queering Contemporary Asian American Art*. Seattle: University of Washington Press, 2017.

Lima, Manuel. *Visual Complexity: Mapping Patterns of Information*. New York: Princeton Architectural Press, 2011.

McCarthy, Andrea. *Ambient Television: Visual Culture and Public Space*. Durham: Duke University Press, 2001.

McInnis, Maurie Dee. *Slaves Waiting for Sale: Abolitionist Art and the American Slave Trade*. Chicago: University of Chicago Press, 2011.

Mirzoeff, Nicholas, ed. *Visual Culture Reader*. 1998; London: Routledge, 2013.

Modleski, Tania. *Loving with a Vengeance: Mass-Produced Fantasies for Women*. 2nd ed. New York: Routledge, 2016.

Mogk, Marja, ed. *Different Bodies: Essays on Disability in Film and Television*. Jefferson, NC: McFarland, 2013.

Moten, Fred. *Black and Blur*. Durham: Duke University Press, 2017.

Mulvey, Laura. *Visual and Other Pleasures*. 1989; London: Palgrave, 2009.

Muñoz, José Esteban. *Disidentifications: Queers of Color and the Performance of Politics*. Minneapolis: University of Minnesota Press 1998.

Pham, Minh-Ha T. *Asians Wear Clothes of the Internet Race, Gender, and the Work of Personal Style Blogging*. Durham: Duke University Press, 2015.

Pollock, Griselda. *Vision and Difference: Femininity Feminism and Histories of Art*. London: Routledge, 1988.

Raiford, Leigh, and Heike Raphael-Hernandez. *Migrating the Black Body: The African Diaspora and Visual Culture*. Seattle: University of Washington Press, 2017.

Sholette, Gregory. *Dark Matter: Art and the Politics of Enterprise Culture*. New York: Pluto Press, 2015.

Siebers, Tobin. *Disability Aesthetics*. Ann Arbor: University of Michigan Press, 2010.

Stavans, Ilan, and Jorge J. E. Gracia, eds. *Thirteen Ways of Looking at Latino Art*. Durham: Duke University Press, 2014.

Stubblefield, Thomas. *9/11 and the Visual Culture of Disaster*. Bloomington: Indiana University Press, 2015.

Sturkin, Marita. *Tourists of History: Memory, Kitsch, and Consumerism from Oklahoma City to Ground Zero*. Durham: Duke University Press, 2007.

Thompson, Krista A. *Shine: The Visual Economy of Light in African Diasporic Aesthetic Practice*. Durham: Duke University Press, 2015.

Vogel, Shane. *The Scene of Harlem Cabaret: Race, Sexuality, Performance*. Chicago: University of Chicago Press, 2009.

Whaley, Deborah Elizabeth. *Black Women in Sequence: Re-Inking Comics, Graphic Novels, and Anime*. Seattle: University of Washington Press, 2016.

Williams, Linda. *Hard Core: Power, Pleasure, and the "Frenzy of the Visible."* Berkeley: University of Californian Press, 1989.

Williams, Linda. *Screening Sex*. Durham: Duke University Press, 2008.

INDEX

Abramović, Marina, 108
Ableism, 95, 156. *See also* Disability
Additivism, 5–6
Aesthetics, 22, 28, 60, 73–75, 90, 141, 158, 173, 183, 187
Agassiz, Louis, 112, 113, 116
Ahmed, Sara, 184, 186
AIDS, 82
Aldrin, Buzz, 139, 140
Algorithmic Justice League, 118
Allahyari, Morehshin, 1–7, 37, 120
Alpers, Svetlana, 62, 64
al-Sufi, Abd al-Rahman ibn 'Umar, 141
Amazonia, 14–16
American Museum of Natural History (New York), 142
An Gyeon, 158, 159
Antarctica, 166–168, 170
Anthropocene, 150–152, 187
Apocalypse, 168–169
Apollo program, 139–141. *See also* NASA
Appadurai, Arjun, 25
Apprich, Clemens, 118
Arcangel, Cory, 13
Armstrong, Neil, 139, 140
Art history, 22–27, 32, 53, 124, 183, 187–188
Artist, 4–5, 12–13, 22–24, 54–55, 57, 149, 187, 188, 189, 190
Art world, 73, 75, 79, 85, 188, 189
Astronomy, and visual culture, 137–147, 165

Aura, 23, 72, 189
Avedisian, Alexis Anais, 6
Azoulay, Ariella, 97, 109, 110

Bailey, Marlon M., 80
Ballroom culture, 80–82, 83, 84
BBC, 16
Benjamin, Walter, 23, 189
Bennett, Tony, 63
Berger, John, 104
Beyoncé (Beyoncé Knowles-Carter), 32–33, 35, 63, 66, 68–71, 72
Bierstadt, Albert, 171, 173
Bishop, Brian, 132–134
Black Lives Matter, 114
Blaxploitation films, 124
Blitt, Barry, 89–94, 124
Bourdieu, Pierre, 25
Brexit, 133
Brooklyn Museum of Art, 54, 55, 64
Brown, Michael, 114
Bruggen, Coosje van, 42
Buolamwini, Joy, 118
Burton, Johanna, 120
Busch, Akiko, 41
Bush, Alex, 167, 168, 170
Bush, George W., 75–76

Canon, 22–26, 32, 188
Carrier, David, 63
Cartwright, Lisa, 25, 29
Chakrabarty, Dipesh, 151
Chicago, Judy, 51–55, 64, 72, 75, 85

Childhood, visual culture of, xiii–xv, xviii, 10, 12, 17–18, 44, 46, 115, 181
Chuh, Kandice, 31
Chun, Wendy Hui Kyong, 164
Clifford, James, 25
Climate change, xxvii, 148–152, 166–170, 187
Clinton, Hillary, 109
Coates, Ta-Nehisi, 113
Consent, 20, 34–35, 103, 106–107, 113
Copeland, Huey, 125
Corporeality, 45, 82, 116–117, 135, 188
Courbet, Gustave, 24
Curry, Ruth, 106
Customs and Border Patrol (US), 18

Dakota people, 44–49
Data, visualization of, 4–5, 13, 117–119, 139–146, 164–165
David, Jacques-Louis, 24
Davis, Angela, 90, 124
Delia (enslaved person), 112–113
Demos, T. J., 161
deSouza, Allan, xxvii, 84
Didi-Huberman, Georges, 96
Disability, 95, 100, 111, 155–156, 169. *See also* Ableism
Documenta, 43, 45
Downton Abbey, 28
Durant, Sam, 41–48, 85

Eisenhower, Dwight D., 163
Enlightenment, 23
Event Horizon Telescope (EHT), 137–138, 145, 147

Facebook, xviii, 18, 76, 79, 100, 108, 190
Fairbanks, Ashley, 49
Fairey, Shepard, 87
Feminism, 22, 26, 53–54, 104, 108–110
#freethenipple, 76
Freud, Sigmund, 188
Fundação Nacional do Índio (Brazil), 14, 16–17
Futurists, xxi

Gaze, 26, 95–96, 98, 104, 108, 118, 125, 188
Gérôme, Jean-Léon, 11
Ghosh, Amitav, 149, 152, 170, 180
Gillibrand, Kirsten, 108
Giotto di Bondone, 24
Global positioning systems, 163–164
Google, xviii, 17, 76–77, 79, 99
Google Earth, 161
Google Street View, 154–157, 160–161, 164
Gore, Al, 150
Greenberg, Clement, 73–74, 189
Guggenheim Museum(s), 65
Gunning, Tom, 116

Haida people, 58, 65
Hall, Stuart, 25
Hamilton, 126–129
Hamilton, Alexander, 126
Han Seok Hyun, 174–177
Haraway, Donna, 22, 152
Hartman, Saidiya, 13, 19, 115
Harvard University, 62, 112–114
Hegarty, Valerie, 170–174, 175
Hegel, Georg Wilhelm Friedrich, 23

Heidegger, Martin, 23
Horrocks, Caitlin, 181, 184

Indigeneity, art world and, 46–49, 58–61, 65, 66, 85
Instagram, 66, 70, 72, 76, 103, 108, 146, 154, 155, 160, 190
ISIS, 3, 4–5

Jackson, Peter, 147
Japanese gardens, xvii
Jay-Z (Shawn Carter), 32–33, 35, 66, 68–71, 72

Kant, Immanuel, 23
Kaplan, E. Ann, 168
Kelley, Michael, 55
Kenny, Jacqui, 154–157, 160–161
Khachiyan, Anna, 6
Kinkade, Thomas, 72–75, 79
Kissinger, Henry, 28
Kitsch, 49, 53, 73–75, 189
Korean scroll painting, 158–160, 164, 177
Kubrick, Stanley, 143

Lacan, Jacques, 188
Landscape, xxvi, 73, 148, 157–160, 164, 170–173, 174–177, 189
Lanier, Tamara, 112, 113, 114, 118
Latour, Bruno, 151
Leonardo da Vinci, 24, 69
Lewis, Sarah, 117
Livingston, Jennie, 83
Louvre (Paris), 32–33, 35, 63, 65, 66, 68–71
Low and high culture, 189. *See also* Kitsch
Lowry, Glenn, 49

Mad Max: Fury Road, 168–169
Madonna (Madonna Ciccone), 83
Manet, Édouard, 123–124
Markle, Meghan, 70–71
Matisse, Henri, 124
McCain, John, 88, 92
McLuhan, Marshall, 22
Mercer, Kobena, 133
Messeri, Lisa, 144, 157
Metropolitan Museum of Art (New York), 28
Miller, George, 168–169
Milner, Greg, 163
Minneapolis Sculpture Garden, 41–49
Miranda, Lin-Manuel, 126–128, 129, 134
Mirzoeff, Nicholas, 29, 34, 97, 121, 122, 141, 152, 191
Mitchell, W. J. T., 10, 12
Mona Lisa, 33, 69–73
Monteiro, Lyra D., 128
Moore, Emily L., 65
Mosul Museum, 3, 4, 7
Moten, Fred, 97
Moxey, Kevin, 24
Murphy, Ryan, 83
Museums, xviii, xxi, xxvi, 3–6, 27–28, 32–35, 41–49, 51–73, 75, 76, 81, 99, 112, 142–143, 175, 181–182, 188, 190

NASA (National Aeronautics and Space Administration), 139–141, 143, 144–145, 162, 165
National Geographic, 16
New Deal, 65
New Yorker, 89–94

INDEX 211

Nixon, Richard M., 28
Nixon, Rob, 170

Obama, Barack, 76, 77, 87–94
Obama, Michelle, 89–94
Ocasio-Cortez, Alexandria, 18, 19
Oldenburg, Claes, 42
Original and copy, 3–6, 23, 36–37, 72, 171, 189–190

Paglen, Trevor, 184
Paris Is Burning, 83
Permission, 16, 19, 68, 79, 112
Picasso, Pablo, 24, 124, 164–165
Pissarro, Joachim, 63
Pollock, Jackson, 24
Pratt, Mary Louise, 25
Public art, 41–49
Pygmalion and Galatea (myth), 10–12

Race, visual culture and, 66–71, 87–94, 95, 112–117, 121–129, 169. *See also* Indigeneity, art world and
Rancière, Jacques, 97
Remnick, David, 92, 93
Renty (enslaved person), 112–113
Rhizome (journal), 4
Rourke, Daniel, 5
RuPaul (RuPaul Andre Charles), 83

Sackler, Elizabeth A., 54
Sadat, Anwar, 28
San Francisco Museum of Art, 51
Satire, visual, 92–93
Schultz, Dana, 115
Selfie, 98–103, 106–107, 109–110, 190

Self-portrait, 98–99, 190
Sholette, Gregory, 85
Sontag, Susan, 96
Space. *See* Apollo program; Astronomy, and visual culture; NASA
Spivak, Gayatri, 151
Springsteen, Bruce, 87, 135
Star Wars, 143
Steinkamp, Jennifer, 130–131
Steyerl, Hito, 36, 37, 126, 134–135
Sturken, Marita, 25, 29
Sulkowicz, Emma, 108–111
Surveillance, 19, 103, 111

Tasker, Sara, 100–101
Thomas, Mickalene, 121–125, 129, 134, 174
Thompson, Krista, 125
3D printing, xviii, 2–6, 190
Till, Emmitt, 115
Till-Mobley, Mamie, 115
Tlingit people, 58, 65
"Treasures of Tutankhamun" (exhibition), 28
Trouillot, Michel-Rolph, xiii, xxiv
Trump, Donald J., 89, 132–133, 134
Twitter, 42, 72, 76, 108, 146
2001: A Space Odyssey, 143

Van Horn, Jennifer, 181–182
Vanilla Ice, 145, 147
Velázquez, Diego, 24
Vertesi, Janet, 165
Viso, Olga, 41, 44, 47, 48–49
Visual atmosphere, xvi, xix, xxiv, xxvii, 30, 50, 80, 120, 182, 184, 186, 190

Visual environment, xiii–xvi, xix,
    xxvi, 29–30, 50, 61, 82
Visuality (the visual), xiii–xxv, 8–13,
    17–22, 25–26, 29–30, 34–36,
    39, 50, 64, 80–81, 84, 95–98,
    100, 134, 152, 184, 191
Vivid Entertainment, 102, 106
Vogue, 28, 83

Walker Art Center (Minneapolis),
    41–49
Wallace, John, 59
Wallace, Scott, 15, 177–178
Ward, Daniel, 181
West, Kim Kardashian, xvi,
    101–107, 110, 111
Whitney Biennial, 115
William Benton Museum of Art
    (Storrs, CT), 68
Williams, Raymond, 25
Wright, Jeremiah, 88

YouTube, 15, 17, 88, 107, 108

Zylinska, Joanna, 165–166

The MIT Press Essential Knowledge Series

AI Ethics, Mark Coeckelbergh
Algorithms, Panos Louridas
Anticorruption, Robert I. Rotberg
Auctions, Timothy P. Hubbard and Harry J. Paarsch
The Book, Amaranth Borsuk
Carbon Capture, Howard J. Herzog
Citizenship, Dimitry Kochenov
Cloud Computing, Nayan B. Ruparelia
Collaborative Society, Dariusz Jemielniak and Aleksandra Przegalinska
Computational Thinking, Peter J. Denning and Matti Tedre
Computing: A Concise History, Paul E. Ceruzzi
The Conscious Mind, Zoltan E. Torey
Contraception: A Concise History, Donna J. Drucker
Critical Thinking, Jonathan Haber
Crowdsourcing, Daren C. Brabham
Cynicism, Ansgar Allen
Data Science, John D. Kelleher and Brendan Tierney
Deep Learning, John D. Kelleher
Extraterrestrials, Wade Roush
Extremism, J. M. Berger
Fake Photos, Hany Farid
fMRI, Peter A. Bandettini
Food, Fabio Parasecoli
Free Will, Mark Balaguer
The Future, Nick Montfort
GPS, Paul E. Ceruzzi
Haptics, Lynette A. Jones
Information and Society, Michael Buckland
Information and the Modern Corporation, James W. Cortada
Intellectual Property Strategy, John Palfrey
The Internet of Things, Samuel Greengard
Irony and Sarcasm, Roger Kreuz
Machine Learning: The New AI, Ethem Alpaydin
Machine Translation, Thierry Poibeau
Macroeconomics, Felipe Larrain B.
Memes in Digital Culture, Limor Shifman
Metadata, Jeffrey Pomerantz

The Mind–Body Problem, Jonathan Westphal
MOOCs, Jonathan Haber
Neuroplasticity, Moheb Costandi
Nihilism, Nolen Gertz
Open Access, Peter Suber
Paradox, Margaret Cuonzo
Phenomenology, Chad Engelland
Post-Truth, Lee McIntyre
Quantum Entanglement, Jed Brody
Recommendation Engines, Michael Schrage
Recycling, Finn Arne Jørgensen
Robots, John Jordan
School Choice, David R. Garcia
Self-Tracking, Gina Neff and Dawn Nafus
Sexual Consent, Milena Popova
Smart Cities, Germaine R. Halegoua
Spaceflight: A Concise History, Michael J. Neufeld
Spatial Computing, Shashi Shekhar and Pamela Vold
Sustainability, Kent E. Portney
Synesthesia, Richard E. Cytowic
The Technological Singularity, Murray Shanahan
3D Printing, John Jordan
Understanding Beliefs, Nils J. Nilsson
Virtual Reality, Samuel Greengard
Visual Culture, Alexis L. Boylan
Waves, Frederic Raichlen

ALEXIS L. BOYLAN is Director of Academic Affairs at the Humanities Institute of the University of Connecticut, where she is also Associate Professor in the Art and Art History Department and Africana Studies Institute. She is the author of *Ashcan Art, Whiteness, and the Unspectacular Man*.